LIGHTNING SKETCHES

As the lightning flashes and lights up the sky from one side to the other, so will the Son of Man be in His day.

ST. LUKE'S GOSPEL

By the same authors

TIME TO ACT

LIGHTNING SKETCHES

by

Paul Burbridge and Murray Watts

HODDER AND STOUGHTON

LONDON SYDNEY AUCKLAND TORONTO

Acknowledgement, front cover:
Roger de Wols from film strip
THE GRAND SLAM

British Library Cataloguing in Publication Data

Burbridge, Paul and Watts, Murray
  Lightning Sketches

ISBN 0–340–26710–0

Dedicated to Richard Everett and Nigel Goodwin, with our gratitude for their friendship and inspiration, and to Andrew, Bernadette, Diana, Dick, Geoffrey, Julie, Nigel and Sarah (the members of Riding Lights Theatre Company, past and present), who have helped to establish this material in performance.

Licence to perform the sketches in this volume

Any performance of a sketch in this volume must be given under licence. This licence refers exclusively to *Lightning Sketches*. (The performance of all theatrical work is governed in a similar way. Normally permission would be granted by the copyright holder for a specific performance or series of performances and payment would have to be made on each occasion, but we have decided to opt for a system of licences given for a period in order to avoid correspondence over each performance of any one sketch.) A licence for *Lightning Sketches* costs £20.00, renewable after three years. It grants the right to perform all the sketches in any context (except on cassette recording, radio, television, video recording and film, where all rights are reserved) and in any combination. It does *not* confer the right to reproduce the text in any form – see publisher's copyright note p. 4 – and acknowledgements should mention title, authors and publishers. Licences may be obtained from '*Lightning Sketches*', St. Cuthbert's Centre, Peaseholme Green, York. All cheques should be made payable to 'Lightning Sketches'. Applications should be made in the name of the church, group or individual that intends to present the material. Licences are not transferable.

The above refers to amateur productions (with paying or non-paying audiences). Any professional company wishing to perform this material, should make a separate application to the same address and this will involve the payment of royalties on box-office takings.

See note on licences (p. 133)

Foreword

by

The Archbishop of York, Dr Stuart Blanch

These *Lightning Sketches* will arrest anybody at some point or other. Perhaps it is my age, but I read, for example, "Eternal Youth" by John Emmett and Andrew Petit, with a certain sense of fellow-feeling for those who are depicted in it. And the next one in the book, "Zacc's for Tax" could hardly be bettered if you are looking for a lightning sketch on the eve of Budget Day. Many a school-teacher too, wearied with his task, could identify himself in "Here Beginneth the Second Lesson".

But perhaps from the point of view of the general reader, who is not contemplating play production, some of the most rewarding sections of the book are the articles which intersperse the plays. Anyone who ever has to speak in public, or write an article, or do a parish magazine, will know only too well the "awful dread of the blank page", which is described and catered for in the article on "Writing Sketches". Every minister of the Gospel, lay or ordained, could profit from the article on "Creating Laughter" – which on the whole we are not good at. In short (and a Foreword must be short), this is an admirable introduction, not only to the art of doing drama but of thinking dramatically – in terms which challenge the actors and the audience alike. Drama is a long-established element in the proclamation of the Gospel down the ages. It remains so to this day, and Paul Burbridge and Murray Watts are to be congratulated on making their skill and experience available to a wider public. The publishers too are to be congratulated on recognising a good thing when they see it.

Stuart Ebor:

Bishopthorpe
York
March 1981

Contents

INTRODUCTION

ONE: *Lightning Sketches* . . . I see. So you think this is a good title for this book?

TWO: Yes, I'm pretty happy with it.

ONE: Good, good – well, let's use it then. Let's go right ahead and use it.

TWO: Do I detect a note of sarcasm, here?

ONE: None whatsoever. I think that *Lightning Sketches* is a marvellous idea for a title, even if it only conveys one very small aspect of this book.

TWO: Which aspect?

ONE: Our capacity for rushed decisions on titles.

TWO: Now look here. We have drunk at least a hundred cups of coffee over this title and there are stains all over my *Roget's Thesaurus* and your *Brewer's Dictionary of Phrase and Fable* to prove it. And, quite frankly, I think that *Lightning Sketches* is a thoroughly comprehensive title.

ONE: Oh yes?

TWO: It conveys speed, light, drama, surprise and clarity.

ONE: Which is more than can be said for a lot of our sketches.

TWO: I'm beginning to find your remarks unhelpful. Anyway, you wrote half of these sketches.

ONE: It's not that half I'm worried about.

TWO: Are you looking for an argument?

ONE: No.

TWO: Yes, you are.

ONE: No, I'm not.

TWO: Look, the point of this title is to give a vivid impression of our aims in writing sketches.

ONE: What are these aims? I've always wanted to know.

TWO: Well, first of all, a clear message – going straight to the point.

ONE: Like a flash of lightning.

TWO: Right. Or exploring themes which clarify a whole area.

ONE: 'Sheet lightning' as opposed to 'forked lightning'.

TWO: You could say that. And don't forget the notion of being charged with electricity – the immense power of drama as a medium of communication.

ONE: Often a shock to the system.

TWO: Possibly. And then there's the double-play on the artist drawing an outline very fast – the 'lightning' sketch – the essence of a portrait, without any superfluous detail.

ONE: You've convinced me.

TWO: Really?

ONE: Yes. This is a marvellous title. All we need now is a book to suit it.

TWO: Look, all we're claiming for this book is that it's a start.

ONE: That was our first book, wasn't it?

TWO: Well, this is another start.

ONE: So you didn't think *Time to Act* was a particularly good start?

TWO: Of course I did. It's because I thought *Time to Act* was a good start that I agreed to write another one with you as a 'follow-on'.

ONE: So it isn't a start, it's a 'follow-on'.

TWO: It's both. Anyway, every new book is a

start of some sort, and the whole idea is
to encourage drama groups to start writing their own sketches and, if they've
been using *Time to Act*, to start moving
towards deeper characterisation and
more demanding material.

ONE: Hence the one or two longer pieces which
would appear to undermine the notion of
'lightning sketches'?

TWO: Only in terms of length, not in terms of
vividness or clarity. Anyway, a half hour
treatment of the conversion of St. Paul
could hardly be called an epic.

ONE: It wouldn't be the first adjective to spring
to mind in describing the material in this
book. Possibly 'episodic'.

TWO: Exactly. Interludes, sketches, pen-por-
traits, playlets, call them what you will.

ONE: Thank you. Well, I'd call the ones I wrote
excellent, pithy, profound and deeply
moving.

TWO: Fine. And what about the sketches we
wrote together?

ONE: I think they're half as good as the ones I
wrote by myself.

TWO: Super. And what about the ones I wrote?

ONE: I think they've been very valuable experience for you.

TWO: Great, great. Well . . . It's been really
marvellous working together . . . By the
way, isn't it about time we took a more
serious tone in this introduction?

ONE: I thought that was the whole point of
asking the Archbishop to write the
foreword.

TWO: What if he writes a screamingly funny
one?

ONE: That could be awkward. One doesn't

bank on Archbishops writing screamingly funny forewords.

TWO: No, one banks on them reassuring the
public that we're very sensible chaps and
we believe what we say.

ONE: Like we are writing this book to the glory
of God and pray that He will use it in the
work of His kingdom.

TWO: Exactly.

ONE: Also that we owe a great debt to David
Watson, rector, and Graham Cray, vicar,
and all the members of St. Michael-le-
Belfrey church, York, for giving us such
powerful encouragement and deep
Christian fellowship.

TWO: You've taken the words out of my mouth.

ONE: And out of the Archbishop's – what's he
going to say in his foreword?

TWO: I've no idea, but we ought to thank him
for saying it.

ONE: Right. And we should definitely thank
him for his encouragement to us, and for
being a patron of Riding Lights Theatre
Company, and for proving his support by
commissioning a new work from us
recently. And for being himself.

TWO: Hear, hear.

ONE: Any more thank yous?

TWO: We'd better watch out or this will start
sounding like the last night speeches at
the local operatic society.

ONE: Don't knock the last night speeches,
they're often more entertaining than the
performance.

TWO: And frequently longer. Who else should
we thank?

ONE: Well, there's our co-director of Riding
Lights Theatre Company, Nigel Forde.

We should thank him for being as crazy as we are, if not crazier, and for permission to include two of his sketches.

TWO: Whilst the prize for the most lightning sketch of all goes to Andrew Petit and John Emmett, stalwarts of the street theatre company Breadrock, for their panoramic vision of 'Eternal Youth'. Chris Norton, of course, unanimously takes the prize for the music.

ONE: And finally – at the risk of sounding sentimental – I think we should say that we love our parents very much and want to thank them for a lifetime of support, love, encouragement and Christian instruction.

TWO: And if people don't like this book –

ONE: They can blame our parents.

TWO: Or, if this seems unfair, they can blame us.

ONE: Right, I think that wraps up the issue of the title – any thoughts on an introduction?

TWO: Maybe we could try doing it as a dialogue.

ONE: Hmm . . . No, I think that's a bad idea.

TWO: Yeah . . . Too self-indulgent, really.

York,
December, 1980

WRITING SKETCHES

If you have ever tried to write a sketch, you will know the Awful Dread of the Blank Page. Pen in hand, you sit staring at the emptiness, willing some idea to form in your head. A clock ticks noisily in the background, reminding you that you have only two hours to produce a sketch on the theme of 'the Israelites' Return from Exile'. Black thoughts enter your head, chiefly about your vicar, who never chooses 'Jonah' or 'Noah' but insists on themes like 'the Fruit of the Spirit' or 'Christian Behaviour'. The top of your pen is beginning to show teeth marks. The page in front of you, however, is still unblemished. The words of John Keats aptly convey your feeling, 'My heart aches, and a drowsy numbness pains/my sense, as though of hemlock I had drunk' and William Shakespeare, 'The native hue of resolution is sicklied o'er/with the pale cast of thought'. Your forehead is now resting on the Jumbo refill pad, which mocks you with its vast, unspoilt whiteness . . . You wake up several hours later, to smile sheepishly at the eager faces of the drama group peering round your door.

If you have not had this experience, or something similar, either you are a genius or you have never written a sketch in your life. Writing – even writing sketches – can be tough going. The most difficult part is sorting out the ideas and beginning to write. Once the page has a few speeches then the rest usually flows much more easily. The purpose of this article, therefore, is to help you approach that early stage of writing a sketch – conceiving the idea, deciding on the form, working out the characterisation and adopting the right language. A clear sense of direction is the best antidote to the mental seizure described above. If you know what you want to achieve and have some idea how to achieve it, the sketch will generate its own momentum: you will follow a logical development from the beginning and have some criterion for accepting and rejecting ideas as you write.

The best way of approaching this subject is to analyse several of the sketches in this book. This makes the authors vulnerable – the sketches are not 'models' but convenient illustrations. Our hope is that you will be encouraged to write better ones. Before looking closely at individual sketches, however, some general points need to be made.

The Idea for a sketch is not such a mysterious phenomenon as it sounds. People often say 'how do you get these ideas?' Or 'I wish I had your imagination', but it is not a magic formula. A subject is chosen, often by a speaker or according to the church calendar. Any subject – however awkward and conceptual – can be dramatised, usually by finding a visual equivalent. 'Apathy' is an abstract subject, but it has definite characteristics. The idea in 'General Conformity' was to dramatise it as an army of apathy looking for potential recruits (see the detailed discussion of how this idea was conceived in the analysis of 'General Conformity' below). The subject of Pilate and Caiaphas, conferring about the crucifixion of Jesus, is so well known that the unusual idea of treating their conversation like a football trainer talking to a football chairman was chosen. In the case of 'Party Games', the subject was the social games people play at cocktail parties and the idea for the sketch was to link this with sports commentaries. The subject for 'The Examination' was the poor biblical knowledge of many Christians and the idea – by inference – was to treat it as a *viva voce* at a university, conducted by devils. 'Spreading the Word Around a Bit' was a dramatisation of gossip in church communities, but the idea was to choose three men (as opposed to the traditional choice of women) and to conclude with the biblical image of 'devouring one another'. In every case the idea for the sketch is influenced by the context (who is the audience?) and the need to avoid clichés: the best way of doing this, particularly when dealing with a familiar subject, is to find a new viewpoint of some kind. An example of this – literally a 'viewpoint' – is 'Angel Space', in which two angels stand at the gates of heaven, look down on the earth and discuss the story of the redemption.

The Form is the next stage, and must be decided before

beginning to write. The choice may be dictated by the context – a very noisy youth club often needs a highly stylised approach (see 'Youth', 'General Conformity' and 'David and Goliath') or at the very least a lively use of comedy ('Zacc's for Tax'). A church service or an evening performance of sketches can sustain a much more naturalistic approach (see 'Early One Morning', 'Question Time'). Sometimes, once the form has been decided, the writing of the sketch follows automatically: this is particularly true of the 'two narrators' style ('An Eye for an Eye', 'In the Nick of Time') or a rhythm style ('David and Goliath'). The first speech prompts the second and so on, whereas a naturalistic form will take longer and requires careful thought about characterisation.

Characterisation is a way of 'earthing' the sketch. The main danger is for it to float in mid-air, with no real sense of place or personality. Where does the action take place? Who are the people? Are they in modern dress? What are their motives? Are they easily hurt, irritable, sceptical, perverse, self-righteous, sympathetic, contradictory, deluded, loving, eccentric? A complex character will have many of these elements and may act unpredictably. If characters are well established, then dialogue will flow much more naturally between them. The writer will find lines suggested because 'This is how X would react to what Y has just said'. Stilted dialogue often means poor characterisation, with the opinions of the writer continually showing through. If a disciple turns to a priest and says 'Do not propagate the structures of your Judaistic religious system to me', you will know that the characterisation leaves something to be desired.

Language needs to be chosen carefully to suit the characters, or the mood of the sketch. What are the special phrases, the rhythms, the dialects, the favourite words of your character? (See discussion of 'Early One Morning' below.) If all the speeches in a play are interchangeable – there are no distinguishing types of language from one character to another – the playwright is being lazy. Even a sketch can suffer from this sort of stereotyped speech, especially if characters are very important. In the case of stylised sketches, accuracy is necessary if there is a parody (see the use of rugby and cricket commentaries in 'Party Games') and in some cases an overall gentleness of language may be appropriate (see the poetic touches in 'Angel Space'). When attitudes are being mirrored, the language must sound familiar (see 'Spreading the Word Around a Bit') or in the case of jargon, very particular terminology needs to be used (Appendix One is an extreme case of this). The language must crystallise the ideas, form and characterisation of the sketch. The choice of the right phrases may be the difference between laughter and boredom, or instant recognition and lack of response. In writing a sketch, it is often worth calling to mind the way your friends, family and colleagues use language. Do they play everything down, referring to a howling wind as being 'a little draughty', or does the man in your office keep on saying 'as you can well imagine . . . as I'm sure you appreciate . . . there is no need for me to tell you . . .? Do your local shopkeepers say 'Me duck', 'Dearie', 'Darling', 'Love', 'Guv'nor', 'Madam', 'Missus', 'Sonnie', 'Sweetheart'? If something good happens is it 'cracker' or a 'nice one', is a person 'dead chuffed', 'knocked out', 'absolutely thrilled to bits', or has it 'really blown his mind'?

There are so many elements in the language around that a good ear and a reasonable memory will provide you with plenty of raw material. Observation will always improve a sketch as it will also help an actor to develop his performance (see note on characterisation in 'Creating Laughter'). So much, then, for general principles. The following analysis of some sketches may help to clarify the practical decisions involved in writing.

Analysing sketches. 'General Conformity' illustrates how a subject, 'apathy', can be developed into an idea. Most ideas develop by a kind of thought association. The first task is to analyse the subject.

What is it? The thought process for 'General Conformity'

worked a bit like this: 'Apathy . . . not caring, doing nothing
. . . crowds of bored people conforming to the ideas of the
majority, drifting along . . . so apathy can mean a kind of
conformity . . . by doing nothing, you become part of a
process . . . apathy is not so much 'dropping out' as 'dropping
in' . . . floating with the tide . . .' This was the seed of an
idea. Apathy – failure to act – is a kind of commitment by
default. It is a kind of conformity. The next stage was to
think of images of conformity, when everyone does the
same thing, 'driftwood, floating downstream . . . mass
production . . . conveyor belts in factories . . . people
watching television . . .' The idea for the sketch has not yet
crystallised but careful analysis and discussion of the subject
has already thrown up several important elements, one
example being the connection with television watching.
Further investigation of the subject suggested the question:
'What makes people conform? Is there some force that
drains them of enthusiasm, leaving them apathetic and
therefore inevitably drifting along with the opinions of
others? The Christian belief in evil powers at work in the
world, scheming to influence man and turn him away from
God, reinforces this notion of a strategy . . . but the influence
of such a force is very subtle . . . through fashion and trends
. . . commitment to Christ is out of fashion . . . but doesn't
this refusal to be involved with religion imply a commitment
to fashion? Fashion can dictate our behaviour . . . dictators
. . . military regimes . . . people in uniform, drilled to
obedience, with no choice or freedom, forced to act in
unison.' The process of thought association is now almost
complete. 'Apathy' has moved all the way to the notion of
an 'army' – this immediately appears paradoxical and
dramatically very fruitful. 'An army of apathy . . . people
drilled into boredom . . . ordered not to take an interest . . .
the general conformity of society could be characterised in
this way . . . General Conformity . . . a useful pun, could be
the name of the dictator who personifies fashion and
controls an army of apathy . . . He could show how mass
opinion, gallup polls, the pressure of the majority, hold

people's minds in a vice-like grip . . .' The image has now been fixed. The message of the sketch is clear. Apathy, and subservience to prevailing opinion, is not a coincidence but a strategy of evil. All that is needed is the application of army commands to the apathetic soldiers and a 'storyline', the obvious one being the attempt to find a new recruit. 'So the sketch centres round General Conformity and his army marching on to the stage to find a new recruit . . . but how could this recruit resist the pressure of General Conformity? . . . By thinking for himself, studying for himself . . . In which case, his beginning to read the Bible could be the signal for the army to arrive in an attempt to dull his senses . . .' The *idea* is now fully established. The *form* of the sketch is simple and 'expressionistic' – a man's spiritual peril is expressed through the device of an army of apathy arriving to press-gang him into conformity. The *characterisation* is basic and stylised. General Conformity is a sergeant-major figure (dramatic licence can happily combine the two ranks in a stylised context); he has a booming voice and a domineering personality. The recruit, 'Trend', is a man-of-the-world, affable but easily influenced. The *language* is thus a simple contrast between military brashness and the hesitant interruptions of Mr. Trend. The comedy lies in commanding people to be apathetic, 'stand with your hands in your pockets and your eyes glazed when you're talking to me. Drop that jaw!' The sketch has now been created in theory and the writing can begin. New thoughts will develop in the process but the final result will be heavily dependent on this careful development of the idea.

This analysis of 'General Conformity' illustrates the importance of a clear grasp of the subject. Everything will flow from turning the subject over and over, looking at every possible facet, digging for images, associating one idea with another and creating unusual combinations. The aim of this 'intellectualisation', strange as it may sound, is simplicity. This will mean the unforgettable communication of a clear idea. Experience shows that talks follow the same principle. A long-winded and confusing talk is often the result of hasty preparation, whereas a disciplined and powerful talk will be the fruit of painstaking study.

'Early One Morning'. The most difficult, if not impossible, moment to dramatise in the gospel story is the resurrection. Writers and film directors have failed for many reasons. One is that the resurrection of Jesus was an extraordinary, unclassifiable event. It changed the course of human history because it was unique. Writers, therefore, are lacking in particular experience of the event and make a serious mistake in concentrating on the sensational aspect of the story – the rolling aside of the stone by angelic forces, earthquakes, flashes of light (each one of these is a favourite with painters). The gospels give no eyewitness account of the actual moment but concentrate on the reactions of individuals to the risen Christ. It is this personal response that is the richest mine for the dramatist. Quite apart from this, a Christian *does* have experience of this aspect of the resurrection and can identify fully with the emotions it arouses. 'Early One Morning' is not an example of 'how to do it' but one of an infinite number of ways that the subject can be approached, given that the reactions of people to the risen Christ are made central. Here, matter-of-fact humour is used to earth the experience and Mary is depicted very much as a local girl with a ready wit rather than a starry-eyed romantic. The danger of the latter is the emotional overkill all too familiar from Hollywood religious epics. The ordinary nature of Mary's characterisation suggested a naturalistic form for the sketch. A simple, believable environment, without stylisation or special effects, is often the best way of dealing with the extra-ordinary events of the gospels. The next task was to create characters who could off-set Mary's experience with their incredulity. The gospel accounts imply that the disciples were slow to believe Mary until they had seen for themselves and so at least one follower of Christ was necessary. Dramatically, this initial reaction of the disciples seemed to symbolise an intellectual belief in Christ without a first hand experience of the risen Lord. This was how the character of Luke developed. Very

little is known of the historical figure and it is obviously
dramatic licence to bring him to Jerusalem so early and to
invent a role for him as Mary's guardian. Nevertheless,
Luke provides an excellent basis for a character (only hinted
at in this sketch). He is remembered as 'the beloved
physician', intensely loyal, and was undoubtedly a man of
letters with an acute scholarly mind. Sometimes the merest
suggestion in the biblical account can give the necessary
inspiration. The idea then developed of giving Luke a
housekeeper, Salome. The name is simply an ironic
reference to the seductive dancer, daughter of Herodias.
Salome in this sketch is anything but that. She is a catalyst
for the action. First of all, she provides some comedy, but
more important, she is a busybody. This means that she can
discuss Mary with Luke and raise issues about Jesus from
the point of view of ignorance and unbelief. Tension is
created between Luke's sympathetic character, believing
but bewildered by the events of the passion, and Salome's
irritating and insensitive comments about Mary and about
Jesus. The tension then shifts at Mary's entrance, when
both characters find themselves in an alliance, faced with
the apparent absurdity of her claim. Through their reactions,
Mary's difficulty in communicating the experience of the
resurrection is made central. This becomes the message of
the sketch (and a comment on any attempt to dramatise the
resurrection): how can such a unique event be understood
without personal experience? Once the *idea*, the *form* and
the *characterisation* for 'Early One Morning' had been
decided, the next issue was the *language*. Clearly all three
people needed ways of speaking that would convey their
characters. Compare Salome and Luke in this opening
sequence:

> SALOME: I knew it would come to this, that's all
> I'm saying.
> LUKE: Quite. You've made your opinion clear.
> SALOME: I mean, that young girl Mary, well . . . It
> doesn't bear thinking of, does it?

LUKE: No, I'm sure you're right there, Salome.
Now if I can just have a few moments
peace?

SALOME: Going off into the night like that to who
knows where, I wouldn't presume to say,
with what she done in her past life . . . A
young girl like that, selling her body for
sex, it's too shocking to mention, all those
men and those –

LUKE: What are you driving at, woman?

SALOME: Well – gone, just like that. Into the night.
I went to clean her bedroom and the bed
wasn't even slept in, imagine that, and all
her best perfumes were gone from the
dresser. And I put two and two together.

LUKE: Yes, I'm sure you did, Salome. Now will
you leave me alone, please?

Luke speaks tersely. There are no qualifying clauses, no
extra adjectives: 'What are you driving at, woman?', rather
than 'My dear Salome, I really cannot understand one single
word, so could you please explain yourself a good deal more
clearly?' In other words, Luke thinks quickly and therefore
comes to the point. He is also tense and preoccupied and not
in the mood to waste words. Salome, by contrast, uses lots
of padding: 'that's all I'm saying', 'I wouldn't presume to
say', 'just like that', 'imagine that'. She begins by speaking
in a circular way, hinting at her meaning. She does not say
'What if Mary has gone back to her life as a prostitute?' She
says, 'I mean, that young girl Mary, well . . . it doesn't bear
thinking of, does it?' When she does make herself a little
clearer in the next speech, she immediately adds 'It's too
shocking to mention' and then proceeds to mention more
details . . . Her speech mannerisms are made a point of
comedy. The first draft of 'Early One Morning' was different
in two ways to this. The character of Salome had not
developed. She was Luke's wife, rather than his housekeeper, and was essentially serious-minded. Very early on she
stated, 'But after all we've done for her, taking her into our

home, caring for her, feeding her, treating her like our own daughter, to leave at three in the morning and go back to that . . . to that horrible brothel . . . to those women.' This was too contrived, directly communicating information without much subtlety. Instead, it is better to let the character dominate rather than the ideas. Salome became more of a gossip. She was given a detached relationship to Luke, which was far more likely to clutch at rumours and notions about what was happening to Mary than the facts. She was also made a comic figure to add a light touch to the beginning, as well as to show that scandal-mongering is more of a reflection on the person who does it than on the character of the victims. The second difference in the first draft was that Luke entered speaking before Salome. His speech ran, 'No, no . . . I refuse to accept it . . . I refuse . . . I . . . there must be something I've overlooked . . . in here, maybe . . . No, I've been through all that and all that . . . so that leaves . . . Oh, it's impossible, Salome, I am getting absolutely nowhere and it is driving me mad, quite mad with frustration.' This was rejected because it started the sketch with Luke's own preoccupation over the events of the passion and his searching the scriptures to find an answer. Dramatically it was 'too heavy'. It is also overstated: 'mad, quite mad with frustration' showed Luke too frenetic. A drier, more disciplined way of speaking was necessary. (Later in the sketch, this dry, rational way of speaking becomes a point of comedy as Luke tries to explain Mary's experience.) Starting the sketch with Salome's speech meant a more immediate beginning. Luke reacts to Salome and all the necessary information emerges through their conversation. Once this early sequence had been created satisfactorily, the sketch was 'set up' for Mary's entrance. In this case, there was no need for several drafts, as the main issues of characterisation and language were now settled. Mary's language is different from both Luke's and Salome's. She is very matter-of-fact. Her first line is simply 'Hello'. She does not rush on stage, shouting 'I've seen Jesus, I've seen Jesus', but starts her account of what happened casually and confidently.

LUKE: I've been searching the scriptures all
night, but no joy – I can't make sense
. . . Why it should have to happen . . . I
don't know why . . . If only He was here
to explain for himself, but . . .

MARY: Yeah, well, I've just seen him in the
garden.

She does not build up emotionally until it becomes
increasingly clear that neither Luke nor Salome believe her.
After Luke's lengthy attempt to explain away her experience,
she cries out with frustration: 'I've just seen Jesus! I've seen
him with my own eyes. Just now. Half an hour ago. He said,
"Hello, Mary." I said, "Hello, Jesus." He was there. I was
there. We laughed and cried. And you won't find that in
your books because it doesn't happen very often.' Even
when she is 'worked up' like this, she still retains her
directness. Her speech mannerisms throughout are casual,
rather than melodramatic: 'I said, "Where've you put the
body?" 'Cos the grave was empty. You know, just a hole.
Just a big black empty hole and no body.' In other words,
she speaks almost like a child, with disarming openness.
Her language is not conditioned by the author's need to
impart information to the audience, so much as by the
demands of her character.

The reason for analysing these sketches is to lay bare
some of the thought processes in creating them and to equip
our readers with techniques and encouragement for devel-
oping their own work. But perhaps the best way of
communicating the theme of this article is to illustrate how
not to do it (unless you feel that we have already done this
. . .) And so, for devotees of disaster movies and lovers of
heroic failures, we include appendix two: 'The Bad
Samaritan' – a sketch where everything can, and usually
does, go horribly wrong. This is also for your encouragement.
Whenever your drama group is at its lowest ebb, just read
this. You will immediately feel that you are making progress.

TELLING THE TRUTH

These sketches are aimed at a general audience. Some of them have been performed in street-theatre ('Youth', 'General Conformity'), others have appeared in revues by Riding Lights Theatre Company ('Party Games', 'The Next Sketch'). They aim to communicate the joy of Christianity and take a critical look at contemporary attitudes.

Angel Space

RAPHAEL, *an Archangel*; HERION, *an angel*

Despite its simplicity, this sketch is quite difficult to perform well. There is little action, so the challenge to the actors is in allowing the vividness of the language to stimulate the imagination of the audience. Many people have an understandably vague conception of supernatural beings, therefore strong characterisation is important. Raphael could be somewhat avuncular, for instance; Herion, wide-eyed and enthusiastic. Perhaps because of its mixture of gentleness, humour and poignancy, this sketch has become one of the most well-loved in this book. It makes the Christmas theme appropriate at any time in the year.

Angel costumes can often provoke unnecessary amusement, so unless something simple and dignified can be found (preferably in pale grey, without wings), the hazard is best avoided altogether in favour of stylised modern dress.
Raphael is discovered on stage. After a pause, Herion enters and without seeing Raphael comes downstage, looking around above the audience, at first cautiously, then with an increasing sense of wonder.

RAPHAEL: What brings *you* to the gates of Heaven, angel?

HERION: (*Surprised at being discovered*) Oh . . . um . . . nothing.

RAPHAEL: Nothing?

HERION: No, I just came outside to look. I'm sorry, I'll go back.

RAPHAEL: Have you never been outside before?

HERION: No. (*Ruefully*) I'm only a minor cherub. I haven't been given my wings yet. But one day soon I hope to fly swiftly at my

Master's bidding – like the others.

RAPHAEL: What is your name?

HERION: Herion. What's yours?

RAPHAEL: Raphael.

HERION: (*Gulp*) Oh, I've never spoken to an Archangel before.

RAPHAEL: What were you looking for?

HERION: Nothing in particular. I've just heard so much about the wonder of all created things, so I wanted to see for myself. I'm not restless or anything, but I meet so many angels returning from flight far and wide in the universe, their eyes almost popping out of their heads as they try to describe what they've seen.

RAPHAEL: I know the feeling. Even when you fly faster than light, you never seem to come anywhere near the end.

HERION: I wish I could go.

RAPHAEL: Well, soon maybe. But you can see quite a lot from where we're standing. I'll show you. (*He comes downstage and gestures upwards, as if throwing back a huge curtain*)

HERION: It's bigger than I could have possibly imagined.

RAPHAEL: It's bigger than you could possibly see. Eternal motion of stars and galaxies. Old ones die and grow cold; new ones burn blue and white like those up there.

HERION: Millions of them. As if a paintbrush, full of light, has been flicked across the sky again and again.

RAPHAEL: And each gap between the stars is a window into distant space beyond. Star after star, their messages still travelling long after they themselves have gone out.

HERION: Oh, wow! (*Pause*) Do Archangels ever feel small?

RAPHAEL: All the time.

HERION: Wouldn't it be great if we could all go on a guided tour of the universe? You could show us round.

RAPHAEL: A lot of us did go out together once . . . when the Son of Almighty God Himself left the splendour of Heaven and went to live on earth for a while. It was a pretty important occasion, so we took the choir along. Filled the sky with singing, just to let them know He'd arrived.

HERION: The people on earth must have loved that.

RAPHAEL: Oh, yes. Made them jump, too.

HERION: Earth must be a fabulous place for the Son of God to go and live there. Is it like Heaven?

RAPHAEL: It used to be, before it was spoilt.

HERION: I bet it's that great big, orange planet up there, 'cos it *is* going a bit pink at the edges, isn't it?

RAPHAEL: No, not that one. You can hardly see it, actually. It's that little dim one down there.

HERION: (*Peering into outer space*) You can't be serious?

RAPHAEL: I am.

HERION: It looks like a chewed-up golf-ball. What in Heaven did He want to go down there for?

RAPHAEL: To help them. To put right what was spoilt.

HERION: Did He rule the earth then?

RAPHAEL: Not in the same way as He now rules with God in Heaven.

HERION: But how did He live? Did you all go and build Him a palace, or something?

RAPHAEL: He was born in a cattleshed, and lived in

various places, wandering . . .

HERION: Born??

RAPHAEL: Yes. As a man.

HERION: You mean He changed into . . . something else?

RAPHAEL: He became very small. Nothing more than a seed – and was born onto the earth.

HERION: How horrible.

RAPHAEL: It was the only way – to help them. But surely you've learnt that about God by now. You spoke of the wonder of all created things: the real wonder is that God cares for each one of them (*Pointing to earth*) that much.

HERION: It's a wonder to me that He didn't come to grief down there on that miserable place.

RAPHAEL: Well, He did . . . and He didn't. But there was a happy ending, as you know.

HERION: Tell me about it.

RAPHAEL: I would if I had time, but 'E'en Eternity's too short' and all that. I must fly. But stay here and watch if you like. (*He exits, leaving* HERION *studying the sky as the lights fade*)

General Conformity

GENERAL CONFORMITY, *supreme commander of the* ARMY OF APATHY (*anything from two to six soldiers*); TREND, *a man of the world*

This is an extract from a full length morality play, THE TRIAL OF TRIMMER TREND, *to be published in due course. Like 'How to be a Hero' from* THE GRAND SLAM, *it stands on its own as a sketch and has been frequently performed by* RIDING LIGHTS. *It is a useful item for street theatre, or for a 'revue' type performance. The* ARMY OF APATHY *should be dressed sloppily and identically.* TREND *is 'discovered on stage reading the Bible' – the beginning of the sketch is sometimes improvised by* RIDING LIGHTS: TREND *enters, holding a Bible, and starts to tell the audience why the book is important and why various sketches have been based on Bible stories. The rest of the sketch then functions like an interruption.*

TREND *thumbs through a Bible. There is the sound of marching.*

TREND: Marching? An army? (*Enter* GENERAL CONFORMITY *and the* ARMY OF APATHY).

CONFORMITY: Hep-by, hep-by, hep-by, hep-by, hep-by, squad, halt. Squad will turn to the right, to the right, turn. Squad will turn on their television sets, by the left, switch. (*The* ARMY *switches on imaginary TVs*) Squad will watch what everyone else watches, eyes front. Now get watching you miserable lot of non-conformists. (*The* ARMY *bend forward, gaping at the screens*)

TREND: Who are you?

CONFORMITY: General Conformity, laddie, and stand with your hands in your pockets and your eyes glazed when you're talking to me.

Drop that jaw. I should hope so. And let's have none of this serious thinking during a routine drill. Whatsyername?

TREND: Trend, sir.

CONFORMITY: Private Trend, I see. Squad, shun! Squad will slope downhill in all matters of personal morality (*They slope to the side*), squad will stand at ease when facing important decisions (*They stand at ease and stare vacantly*), squad will stand easy and do nothing about anything (*They slouch haphazardly*). Private Trend, fall in!

TREND: (*Hedging*) Well, as a matter of fact, I was more or less thinking of following my conscience, you know, investigating the issues of right and wrong for myself by studying the –

CONFORMITY: Private Trend, stand stock still! Squad! Squad shun! Squad will retire one pace, by the left, re-tire! (TREND *finds himself in the army by doing nothing*)

TREND: I feel I ought to . . . go . . . my own way, do what I think . . . follow what my conscience tells me –

CONFORMITY: YOU PATHETIC LITTLE MUMMY'S BOY OF A RELIGIOUS NUTCASE!! (*Seeing the Bible tucked under* TREND's *arm*) 'Ello, 'ello, what's this, what's this? (*He takes it*) The *Bible*.

TREND: (*Deprecating*) Oh – is it? Oh, my goodness me.

CONFORMITY: Oh dear, oh dear, you've got it coming to you, laddie, if your friends were to find out that you were reading a book like this, laddie, you could be sentenced to up to two hours public embarrassment.

TREND: Yessir.

CONFORMITY: From now on you will not read this book, laddie.

TREND: Nossir.

CONFORMITY: Why will you not read this book, laddie?

TREND: Don't know, sir.

CONFORMITY: Well done, private Trend, well done. You don't know why you will not read this book, laddie?

TREND: Nossir.

CONFORMITY: BECAUSE NOBODY ELSE DOES. THEY JUST DON'T, LADDIE. Is that clear?

TREND: Right, sir.

CONFORMITY: Right. SQUAD WILL FOLLOW THE FASHION!

ARMY: (TREND *joins in*) Sah!

CONFORMITY: SQUAD WILL BELIEVE WHAT THE EXPERTS TELL THEM!

ARMY: Sah!

CONFORMITY: SQUAD WILL NOT INVESTIGATE FOR THEMSELVES!

ARMY: Sah!

CONFORMITY: (*To* TREND) Don't let me catch you stepping out of line again or you'll be thoroughly ridiculed, is that clear, number 892?

TREND: Sah!

CONFORMITY: And wipe that look of rapt attention off your face when you're talking to me! Next time, I expect to see a marked decrease of interest and a pretty good display of apathy. SQUAD, APATHET-ICALLY, MARCH. (*Exeunt, slouching and yawning in unison*) Let's have more conformity there . . . I want a lot less personality in this squad . . .

Eternal Youth   *by John Emmett and Andrew Petit*

TWO MEN, *hearty keep-fit fanatics, somewhat out of condition*

Clearly, the most lightning sketch in this book. An excellent opener to a programme, especially in street theatre, where a fast, noisy, 'physical' beginning helps to start gathering a crowd. Unless otherwise indicated, the dialogue should be accompanied by a continuing routine of physical jerks, running on the spot, press-ups etc., which gradually winds down at the end of the sketch, as the two men struggle to keep the illusion of youthfulness alive in the face of creeping decrepitude.

They approach the stage area at a jog, puffed and perspiring, dressed in absurd P.T. kit, encouraging each other with several 'Hup, two, three, fours' etc. They reach the stage and set about their own training programmes.

> ONE: (*Thumping chest*) Yup, I reckon that's a pretty good body I've got there!
> TWO: Tireless legs.
> ONE: Massive biceps.
> TWO: Barrel chest.
> ONE: Trim waist.
> TWO: Shining eyes.
> ONE: Glossy coat.
> TWO: Wet nose.
> ONE: Pot belly.
> TWO: What? (*They pause to study the unwanted pounds*)
> ONE: Oh, well, never mind.
> TWO: I like my beer. (*Pulling a pint*)
> ONE: Enjoy yourself while you're young.
> TWO: Thank goodness we're young.

ONE: Have a good time with the chicks.

TWO: But don't get tied down.

ONE: Not unless you love her.

TWO: I love my girl. (*Assumes romantic pose*)

ONE: So do I.

TWO: What?

ONE: (*Laughing it off*) Marriage is great.

TWO: When you're young.

ONE: No kids yet, mind you.

TWO: Keep you're freedom.

ONE: But there comes a time,

TWO: When you need a family.

ONE: It's fun if you're young.

TWO: Little baby, just like his mum.

ONE: Little daughter, just like me.

TWO: It's lovely to watch them grow up.

ONE: If you're still young.

TWO: They've left home now (*Waves*),

ONE: So we're free again! (*Over-exerts himself and injures hamstring*)

TWO: And we're young.

ONE: (*Rubbing leg*) I've had to give up soccer, though.

TWO: Haven't got the time.

ONE: I prefer a more mature game.

TWO: But we're still young.

ONE: Young enough to play cricket. (*They do the appropriate actions, becoming increasingly senile and arthritic*)

TWO: Or golf.

ONE: Or croquet.

TWO: Bowls.

ONE: Or tiddlywinks.

TWO: Or scrabble. (*They now look more like a couple of ancient dogs, digging for bones*)

BOTH: But we're still young. ERRG-GAAAGGGHH! (*They die*)

Zacc's for Tax

ZACCHAEUS; TWO MEN, *in the queue at the tax office*; WIDOW; CROWD, *up to a dozen extras*; JESUS

The story of ZACCHAEUS *is always popular with children and adults, and in the case of this sketch, particularly with street theatre audiences.* JESUS *had a special affection for the odd person out, and this story shows the joyous scope of the Gospel – everyone is included.*

This sketch requires vigorous, yet disciplined crowd participation and a strong individual performance from both ZACCHAEUS *and* JESUS. *Centrestage there is a table, displaying a sign which says, 'Zacc's for Tax'. The crowd enters and mills around, grumbling and complaining in the way people usually do in Tax Offices. After a while,* ZACCHAEUS *enters this rather hostile atmosphere.*

ZACCHAEUS: All right, All right. I'm sorry I'm late, but you've got to remember this is a government department. Now form an orderly queue. Who's first?

1ST. MAN: I was here first.

ZACCHAEUS: Good morning, sir. You haven't been here for a long time, have you?

1ST. MAN: Er, no.

ZACCHAEUS: So, take out your wallet, open it and say after me, 'Help yourself.'

1ST. MAN: Help yourself. (ZACCHAEUS *does so*) Hey, wait a minute, you can't just take my money!

ZACCHAEUS: That's very kind of you, sir, what else are you offering?

1ST. MAN: Look, I'm entitled to allowances. I've got a rebate . . . are you forgetting –?

ZACCHAEUS: You're right. I am forgetting one thing –
V.A.T.

1ST. MAN: V.A.T.? What's that?

ZACCHAEUS: (*Whipping a dagger*) Voluntary Additional
TIP. (*The man grudgingly obliges*) Next?
Ah, it's you is it, sir? Let's see. (*Leafing
through long legal document*) It says here
under Fiscal Adjustments, page 20, para-
graph 8, unearned earnings, subsection
14k, the aforementioned is liable under
clause 4 to the bdabda bda . . . of the
aforementioned regional paycode men-
tioned earlier and hereinafter the under-
signed. I'm afraid I'm going to have to do
you for Shoe Tax, House Tax, Camel
Tax, Head Tax, Syntax, Tin Tacks and
Carpet Tacks.

2ND. MAN: 'Ang on, what's Head Tax?

ZACCHAEUS: That's a new one on you, is it, sir? Well,
let me explain. Head Tax is the circum-
ference of your head, unfortunately for
you, sir, multiplied by today's percentage
fall on the Stock Exchange, as it affects
me, which in the case of your head, sir,
(*Rapidly using calculator*) comes to sixty-
seven shekels.

2ND. MAN: Sixty-seven shekels!!

ZACCHAEUS: It *is* an awkward figure, isn't it, sir? Why
don't we round it up to a straight hundred.

2ND. MAN: (*Pleased by this concession*) Thank you
very much. (*He pays up, realises his
mistake; is about to remonstrate*)

ZACCHAEUS: Next. Ah, madam. And what is the
number of your P.A.Y.E. tax code?

WIDOW: I'm sorry, I don't know.

ZACCHAEUS: What does your husband earn?

WIDOW: He died three months ago.

ZACCHAEUS: I'm sorry to hear that. Well, what did he

earn before he . . . before.

WIDOW: I don't know. He was a roadsweeper.

ZACCHAEUS: Ah, Council, was he? Well, that's probably about six hundred shekels a year. I'm sorry, I'm going to have to charge you at the old rate, for the whole period. I mean, it wouldn't do for the Chief Tax Collector to be caught bending the rules, would it? (*By this time he is getting quite a bit of barracking from the crowd*) So that's, er, forty-eight shekels.

WIDOW: It's no wonder what they say, is it?

ZACCHAEUS: What's that, then?

WIDOW: You haven't got no friends. (*The crowd are in an ugly mood. They move in on* ZACCHAEUS *threateningly*)

ZACCHAEUS: (*Nervously jocular*) Friends? Ha ha, who needs friends? Now, come on, ladies and gents, keep back. Let the dog see the rabbit . . . (*They might well be about to lynch him, when one person sees* JESUS *approaching the stage from the audience.*)

VOICE: Well, will you look at that, will you? There's Jesus? (*The crowd immediately rush to the front of the stage cheering and waving, inviting Jesus to come and tell them a story etc. In the ensuing chaos,* ZACCHAEUS *is repeatedly pushed aside so he goes and climbs a 'tree'. A stepladder will do. He joins in the shouting*)

ZACCHAEUS: Hello, Jesus! I can see you. Jesus, Jesus! (JESUS *stops some way off, staring at* ZACCHAEUS. *Noticing this, the crowd falls silent. They also turn to stare at* ZACCHAEUS, *who is still shouting*) Hello, Jesus! I can see yer, mate. Come over here. Tell us a story. It's – gone very quiet all of a sudden. What's the matter with you lot?

Don't mind me, I just happen to like
climbing trees, that's all. There's no law
against climbing trees, is there? Just 'cos
I'm short. No law against being short,
either. Is there a law against being short,
I ask myself, and what do I reply? No,
course there isn't. So don't look at me,
then. You're supposed to be looking at
Jesus. Well, he's over there, isn't he? Go
on, look at him, 'cos he's – what's he
looking at? Nothing else up here, is
there? 'Allo? 'Allo?

JESUS: Zacchaeus!

ZACCHAEUS: Who said that? Who said my name?
Come on, somebody said my name? I
mean, it's not unreasonable to presume
that I am the only person called Zacchaeus up this particular sycamore tree.

JESUS: Zacchaeus!

ZACCHAEUS: There you are, it was . . . Jesus. Can't be.
Not Jesus. Not talking to me. I mean,
I'm a bad lot, aren't I? (*The crowd murmur
their agreement*) I'm a fiddler and a
diddler, a rake and a rip-off. I'm a thief.

JESUS: Zacchaeus, if you don't hurry up, you're
going to be late.

ZACCHAEUS: Am I?

JESUS: Yes.

ZACCHAEUS: What for?

JESUS: Tea.

ZACCHAEUS: Oh, tea. What do you mean, tea?

JESUS: I'm coming to your house for tea.

ZACCHAEUS: Are you?

JESUS: Yes. Didn't you know?

ZACCHAEUS: No. How did you know?

JESUS: I've just decided to.

ZACCHAEUS: But you can't just come round like that. I
haven't done the washing up. This month.

JESUS: I don't want to see your house, Zacchaeus, I want to see you.

zacchaeus: But maybe there are lots of things about me that I wouldn't want you to see, see? Like all that wrong. (*Approving murmurs from crowd*) and all that fiddling and all that money and . . . I'll tell you what, I'll give it all back! (*Gasp from crowd*) No, I won't. (*Groan*) I'll give back four times as much! To anyone I've robbed, I'll give back four times as much! (*The crowd are ecstatic,* ZACCHAEUS *tumbles down and rushes up to* JESUS) Hey, Jesus, are you really coming to my house for tea?

JESUS: Yeah.

ZACCHAEUS: (*Barely controlling his delight*) To *my* house?

JESUS: Your house.

ZACCHAEUS: Heyheyhey!!! (*Unsure for a moment*) No kidding?

JESUS: No kidding.

ZACCHAEUS: (*Gives triumphant yell*)

JESUS: Zacchaeus, today salvation has come to you!

Here Beginneth the Second Lesson   by Nigel Forde

MR. FLETCHER, *a teacher of Ancient History, middle-aged, slightly stuffy, thinks he is one of the lads;* CULSHAW, *a schoolboy. Lazy but very bright; the bane of every teacher's existence;* SAMANTHA, *will one day be a hairdresser;* DOREEN, *quite bright but a bit of a plodder; admires Culshaw immensely;* BRISTER, *can just about spell 'and'; sometimes sits the right way up but seldom moves.*

The main thing to beware of in this sketch is lack of discipline among those playing the school children. Theoretically, any number of extra actors can be used to fill out the class, but the danger of upstaging the action is thereby increased. In many ways it takes more experience to play a bit-part than a main character. It is a fairly static sketch – the only actor who can move is he who plays the teacher – and the point of the sketch is lost if the arguments are not clearly presented; so pace and energy, though important, must not obscure the dialogue. It is not a sketch which works well in schools; it is best performed for that age-group in an out-of-school environment, and best of all to a mixture of adults and young people.

The pupils' chairs are placed facing downstage and towards centre stage. The teacher's desk is similarly placed but on the other side. The pupils are waiting for the lesson to start; giggling, chattering discussing last night's TV etc. Brister is deep in thoughtlessness. Mr. Fletcher strides in looking rather the worse for wear. He bangs his briefcase on his desk. No one takes any notice. As he yawns and pulls himself together the class quietens down and looks at him expectantly.

FLETCHER : Morning, everybody.
     ALL : (*With varying degrees of sing-song lethargy*)
          Morning Mr. Fletcher.

FLETCHER: Right. Now. We're going to carry on this morning with our study of the staff room. (*There is a small murmur of bafflement*)

CULSHAW: D'jer what, sir?

FLETCHER: (*Bringing out his joke*) Life in the Ancient World, Culshaw!

DOREEN: Oh, it's a joke.

CULSHAW: (*Reassuringly*) Must be Wednesday.

FLETCHER: (*Who hasn't heard or takes no notice*) Now, on Monday last we looked briefly at Christianity and the birth of Jesus of Nazareth. What did we discover about his actual birthday? Samantha?

SAMANTHA: (*Waking from her daydream*) Er . . . that he was not born in the year nought, sir. (*The class is fairly surprised*)

FLETCHER: Yes. Good. We can't be sure when he was born actually, but it was almost certainly *after* the year nought, which of course puts a big question-mark over whether he was born at all. (*It takes a moment for this magnificent illogicality to sink into the class, but from this point begins* CULSHAW'S *determined attack on* FLETCHER'S *credibility*) Now, much more interesting from our point of view, is the remnant of another belief, another philosophy – the Stoic philosophy, which we find . . .

CULSHAW: (*Hand up, excited*) Sir, sir!!

FLETCHER: (*Wearily*) What is it, Culshaw?

CULSHAW: Sir, there's a woman walking across the football pitch, sir! (*The class is delighted at something of real interest but quietens immediately* FLETCHER *speaks*)

FLETCHER: (*Icily*) I am sure we are all indebted to Culshaw for his profound and helpful

remarks on the peripatetic qualities of
the female biped . . .

CULSHAW: But when was she born, sir?

FLETCHER: How the hel . . . (*Pulling himself together
with dignity*) I have no means of discovering that, Culshaw.

CULSHAW: But that puts a big question-mark over
whether she was born at all, (*Innocently*)
doesn't it sir?
(*There is a pregnant pause*)

FLETCHER: On page 46 we find a brief outline of Stoic
philosophy. It was popular with many
people. It is a fine belief – strong, stark,
courageous . . .

CULSHAW: But was it true, sir?

FLETCHER: Culshaw, I am beginning to find these
interruptions irritating. Was *what* true?

CULSHAW: What the Stoics believed, sir.

FLETCHER: I don't think I quite understand what
you're getting at, Culshaw.

CULSHAW: (*Butter wouldn't melt in his mouth*) Sorry,
sir. I just wondered whether they believed
in strong stark courageous truth . . . or a
load of noble codswallop – sir.

FLETCHER: (*Rescuing what he can from the situation*)
Ah! So Culshaw knows what truth is!
Well, well, well! Ladies and gentlemen of
5B, this is an historic day . . .

CULSHAW: I dunno that I do know what truth is, sir.
I just wondered if you did?

FLETCHER: (*Caught off guard*) Truth? Ah . . . er . . .
well . . . truth is . . . ahem . . . truth is
what is ultimately . . . um . . . something
which . . . er . . .

DOREEN: (*Who looked it up last week and recites*)
Something which outlasts fashions and
civilisations and remains whether anybody cares about it or not.

(*Even* CULSHAW *is impressed.* FLETCHER
flounders)

FLETCHER : Er, yes. Thank you Doreen: well put.
That's it. The unchangeable, the basis of
the universe.

CULSHAW : (*Relentlessly*) So it wasn't true, then sir?

FLETCHER : (*Patiently*) What wasn't?

CULSHAW : (*Overreaching himself for once*) Stogie tism
. . . stosket . . . what you said sir: them
ancient beliefs.

FLETCHER : That would be a very rash assumption,
Culshaw.

CULSHAW : (*Supported by the class*) No, sir! You said!
If no one believes it any more, if it hasn't
lasted then it can't be the truth.

ALL : Yeah. That's right sir. You said. Come
on, Fletch. Etc, etc.

FLETCHER : (*Quietening them down genially*) Yes, yes,
all right . . . in a way. But remember, my
learned friends, there are many aspects
of Stoic belief in that Christianity you're
all so fond of. Of course it is the central
core of Christianity that is so different
and so difficult . . .

SAMANTHA : Sir, just 'cos it's difficult doesn't mean to
say it's wrong!

FLETCHER : (*Bringing out his trump card*) Really
Samantha? Well, I should have thought
that, if all men were supposed to believe
and accept it, it should be extremely *easy*
to understand.

DOREEN : Why do you say that about Christianity,
sir?

SAMANTHA : Yeah, you don't say it about anything
else.

CULSHAW : Things which you happen to know are
true.

SAMANTHA : Things which *you* believe.

FLETCHER: Oh really? Such as what?

DOREEN: Well, arithmetic, sir, and technical drawing.

SAMANTHA: Biology.

BRISTER: Physics.

(*There is a moments pause as all turn to gaze at* BRISTER *with awe and wonder. Then back to the fray*)

SAMANTHA: Yeah, just because electricity is hard to understand, doesn't mean it isn't true.

DOREEN: Sir, you're always saying things need a bit of effort (*And here she quotes him. The others join in as they recognise it*) Nothing great was ever achieved without hard work.

FLETCHER: (*He is embarrassed*) Yes, yes, yes, all right.

SAMANTHA: Well, there you are, sir. Why should it be different when it comes to learning about God?

FLETCHER: Well, I'll tell you, Samantha. You see, all the basic questions about physics, astronomy, geonomy, physiognomy and so onomy ... er ... so on, have been answered and, what's more, been proved to be true *by experience*. Now there are some very basic questions about God which cannot be answered.

CULSHAW: There are some very basic questions about cancer, sir, like how and why. But that doesn't stop people dying from it.

DOREEN: Sir, you said it was important to prove things by experience; well, there's a lot of people who have proved Christianity by experience. Why don't you believe them?

FLETCHER: That's very simple – I haven't had the experience myself.

CULSHAW: 'Ere, has Mr. Fletcher ever been up in a rocket?

SAMANTHA: (*Wondering what he is getting at*) No.

CULSHAW: Ah, so he doesn't believe in space-travel.

DOREEN: (*Catching on*) Has he ever fallen under a tube train?

SAMANTHA: (*Enjoying this*) No!

DOREEN: So – he doesn't believe in electrocution then!

SAMANTHA: Hang on! Has he ever been to Greece?

DOREEN: Don't think so.

CULSHAW: Oh dear, so that probably doesn't exist either.

SAMANTHA: I wonder why he bothers to teach us about it?

DOREEN: It's awful when you think what he's missing.

SAMANTHA: Yeah, shame really!

DOREEN: I mean, he doesn't believe in the Indian Ocean, Battle of Waterloo, Oxygen . . .

CULSHAW: Brain surgery, radio waves, childbirth . . .

DOREEN: Igloos, kangaroos. . . .

FLETCHER: (*Who has had enough*) All right, all right, that'll do. This is all getting rather silly and the arguments are fatuous.

CULSHAW: (*Quickly*) Yeah, well they're all based on your reasoning, sir.

FLETCHER: (*Grasping his ear and giving it a tweak*) Look, Culshaw, you stupid little boy; I can read books, understand historical documents and believe what intelligent people tell me.

CULSHAW: Yeah. Always excepting The Bible, the Dead Sea Scrolls and the Archbishop of Canterbury.

FLETCHER: Yes. NO!! Um, that's different. It can't be proved.

DOREEN: Any more than anything else. Right!

FLETCHER: All right.

OK. (*He is quiet and very much in control*

of his mounting impatience. But he's got them now) You prove to me, you *prove* to me, that Jesus of Nazareth actually existed.

(*The room falls quiet as* Culshaw *takes up the challenge*)

CULSHAW: You prove to me that your great-granny actually existed.

FLETCHER: Well . . . that's easy; I've got her birth-certificate.

DOREEN: Forged.

FLETCHER: (*Disconcerted. He tries again*) And . . . and photographs. Plenty of photographs.

SAMANTHA: Fakes.

FLETCHER: (*With the quiet certitude of desperation*) Look, there are lots of people who actually remember her.

CULSHAW: (*Quietly but finally*) They're lying.

FLETCHER: I've got diaries!

ALL Oooooh. Tut tut!

SAMANTHA: Very unreliable sources.

DOREEN: Subjective.

SAMANTHA: Biased.

CULSHAW: Emotional.

FLETCHER: (*Not even trying to remain calm any more*) Look, this is ridiculous! How can I prove anything if you constantly disallow the evidence?!

CULSHAW: (*With mock surprise*) Isn't that funny, sir? That's exactly what I would have said about Jesus. Oh – there is just one other thing I could bring up as proof, since you say things can be proved by experience.

FLETCHER: (*Pause. But he is interested despite himself*) Well?

CULSHAW: (*After a long pause, without removing his eyes from* FLETCHER) I've met him.

Short Cut to Nowhere

HEROD, *king of the Jews* ; HERODIAS, *his wife* ; SOCIETY PEOPLE ;
JOHN THE BAPTIST

*'Short Cut to Nowhere' is a musical sketch, perhaps the logical
development of the rhythm style in 'David and Goliath' and
'The Parable of the Good Punk Rocker' in* Time to Act. *It is
simple and 'expressionist' – using a central image and a highly
stylised form.* HEROD *and* HERODIAS, *clad in expensive clothes,
stand centre stage.* HEROD *holds a steering wheel and mimes
driving along the motorway as he and* HERODIAS *sing together.
Soon, they are joined by others, among them doctors, bankers,
teachers, poets, preachers (no limit on numbers), all of them
holding steering wheels and 'driving' straight ahead. They are
all convinced that they are following the right road.* JOHN THE
BAPTIST *arrives, dressed in crash helmet, goggles, covered in
badges saying 'danger', 'hazard', 'stop', 'halt at major road
ahead' etc. He is a jarring intruder, both to their moral
complacency and to the style of their light opera. He sings
harshly, like the lead singer of a new wave band. His warnings
of disaster go unheeded and they brush him aside. The sketch
ends when the music suddenly breaks off: all the* SOCIETY
PEOPLE, HEROD *and* HERODIAS *mime approaching disaster,
crash and death. They fall silently to the floor. Although* Riding
Lights *has produced a number of musicals, musical sketches
are a recent experiment. Sung well and performed well, they
can add to the diversity of an evening as well as drawing on the
musical skills of a group – which are often more general and
more advanced than acting skills. Besides this, rhythm and
memorable tunes, accompanied by very simple images, linger
for a long time in an audience's memory. 'Short Cut to Nowhere'
is essentially a sketch for an adult audience – both the message,
and the parody of the light opera, will tend to go over the heads
of a young audience. (Whereas 'David and Goliath', written for
children, is eminently suitable for adults, such flexibility is often*

disastrous the other way round). The style of this sketch, when compared with one on the same subject in Time to Act *('Keep on Keeping on'),* shows how differently a simple theme can be handled.

SHORT CUT TO NOWHERE

WATTS/NORTON

For the Good of the Team   *by Nigel Forde*

CAIAPHAS, *a football trainer, weak, worried but aggressive;*
PILATE, *a football chairman, powerful, needs success.*

*Like all sketches which say one thing in terms of another, this
sketch treads a delicate tightrope between illumination and
obscurity. It is deceptively easy and needs careful direction; but
if it is acted with real conviction and not allowed to fall into
caricature it can be quite chilling. It is extremely important that
the first four words be clearly heard!*

CAIAPHAS *enters; he is slightly nervous. Despite his ambition
and determination he is never quite sure of how to handle
PILATE. He does a few casual warm-up movements to calm his
nerves, but stops immediately PILATE enters. PILATE comes in
swiftly. Sun glasses, big tie, coat collar up. He possesses the
stage. The rest of the movement in the sketch belongs almost
entirely to CAIAPHAS.*

> PILATE: Morning Caiaphas.
> CAIAPHAS: Morning Pilate.
> PILATE: I hope you've got something important to
> say. I've a lot of work on. Where are the
> others?
> CAIAPHAS: It's . . . um . . . it's just you and me, sir.
> PILATE: (*Patronisingly*) I'm intrigued.
> CAIAPHAS: A bit of trouble with the team.
> PILATE: I thought it was doing very well.
> CAIAPHAS: (*Quickly, to preclude criticism*) Ah, yes! In
> a manner of speaking, it is. Yes.
> PILATE: (*Patiently*) Well then?
> CAIAPHAS: (*Not quite knowing how to begin*) Well, sir
> . . . a team, you see sir . . . it's . . . well, it's
> a team, isn't it?
> PILATE: Devastating, Caiaphas.

CAIAPHAS: I mean, you can't have someone in a team who's . . . who's different. I expect you know who I'm talking about.

PILATE: I could hazard a guess. From what I hear he is very good.

CAIAPHAS: (*Playing for time*) Well, it all depends on . . .

PILATE: He's original.

CAIAPHAS: (*Grudgingly*) Oh, yeah, well I suppose . . .

PILATE: Creative, unselfish.

CAIAPHAS: (*Still unwilling to concede a point*) Yes, you could say . . .

PILATE: He inspires the rest of them and he gets results. What's wrong with that?

CAIAPHAS: (*Suddenly savage*) He doesn't play it by the book!

PILATE: (*Quickly*) Fouls?

CAIAPHAS: Well, no; not exactly fouls, no. But he doesn't play the way I want the team to play. Look, this team has got a history, a tradition to live up to . . .

PILATE: And that doesn't include doing well . . .?

CAIAPHAS: (*Firmly*) No! (*Suddenly realising what he has said*) I mean yes! I mean . . .

PILATE: You mean he is just too good for you. He knows more about the game than you do and you don't like it.

CAIAPHAS: The rest of the team can't live up to him. Look, I've got to train them, haven't I? That's my job. How can I tell them one thing when he goes out there and does something entirely different?

PILATE: And gets results. Look, the fans love him, don't they?

CAIAPHAS: (*Disgusted*) Oh, the fans, the fans; what do they matter? (*Ingratiatingly*) I'm thinking of the team. Individual skills are all very well, but it's teamwork that counts.

He shows everybody up; he's got to go!

PILATE: (*Putting* CAIAPHAS *in his place*) And you're going to get rid of him.

CAIAPHAS: (*Laughing off his embarrassment*) Ah . . . no, well . . . you see, I can't. Can I? *You* can, being on the board and that . . .

PILATE: Which is why I am here. (*Bringing the conversation to a close*) Well, I don't see the problem. I can't fault him.

CAIAPHAS: (*Quietly, almost casually*) He's, er . . . he's after the boss's job, of course.

PILATE: (*Suddenly alert. Urgently*) He's what?

CAIAPHAS: Stands to reason, dunnit? He's going to cause a division. It's his style or the boss's style. (*He feels that at last he has the upper hand and spells it out quietly and deliberately*) Loyalties will change.

PILATE: (*Without admitting anything*) So, what do you want me to do? Free transfer?

CAIAPHAS: No, no, no. He'll be a troublemaker wherever he goes; bring the whole game into disrepute.

PILATE: What then?

CAIAPHAS: (*Quietly*) Just . . . er, just suspend him for a while (*Pause*) if you get my meaning . . . ?
(*They remain motionless as the lights slowly fade*)

The Next Sketch

THREE INTRODUCERS

This sketch is a carefully rehearsed organisational bungle. No apology is made for the obvious lack of spiritual content here and the reader would be ill-advised to try and puzzle out the theology of this piece. It is designed as a 'filler' to come about number four or five in an evening of sketches, where the presence of a compère has already been established, though at this point three compères turn up, each having been privately invited to go on and introduce the next sketch. None of them is aware of this over-efficiency until they are on stage. The experience rapidly becomes a nightmare. All three move and speak in exactly the same way at exactly the same time, which is, of course, extremely hard to do and requires repeated rehearsal and absolute attention to detail – expression, gesture, tone. With subtlety and performed as a perfect clockwork routine, this sketch can be hilarious and have a sleepy audience on the edge of their seats in thirty seconds flat. Use it with skill and discretion.

Three people enter from different points and come straight to the front of the stage. Any combination of men or women will do; two men, with a woman in the middle is possibly best. Their initial confidence is unnerved and passes through stages of embarrassment and frustration towards complete madness. They stand equidistant.

> TOGETHER: The next sketch we'd like to do f . . . . or
> you – (*The attempt to establish a pleasant rapport with the audience is cut short as each is suddenly aware of the other two. They look at each other. There is a note of warning in the voice.*) I'm introducing this one. (*With tight laugh to audience*) At

least, I thought I was. (*More embarrassed laughter, ending in empty gesture of clapping hands together. Notice this. Laugh again.*) No, really, I am!!. (*Hesitate*) . . . I think. (*A forced smile to audience. Freezes, whispering through clenched teeth.*) It's all right, I'll do it. Set the chairs or something. (*Small peremptory gesture*) Get off! (*Trying to regain composure. To audience.*) I'm sorry about all this. There's obviously been some mistake, but never mind. (*A quick nervous glance at others.*) Well, the next (*Sudden pause*) sketch is about – (*Pause. With increasing volume and pace*) Look, I must apologise, I don't know what on earth these two people think they're doing, it really isn't my fault. Oh, shut up will you, the next sketch follows on SHUT UP directly from what you've just seen – LOOK. (*Walking sharply towards each other, meeting in a close huddle centrestage. Whispering maniacally*) if you don't shut up this minute . . . there are people (*Three fingers point at audience*) watching this, you know! (*Silence. Glares. Back to position*) I wuh – OH, FOR GOODNESS SAKE!!! (*Give up. Stalk off stage. Check before disappearing, as if to catch others out and sneak back alone. See others have stopped too. Think better of it*) No. I'm going. (*Slow turn with despairing finality. Suddenly turn all the way round and rush back to front. Pause*) Tomorrow, you'll be painting scenery. (*Panic*) You two are *mindless robots*! (*Quietly, with sudden inspiration*) Bet you can't say, 'Betty Botter bought a bit of better butter . . .' (*Groan*) . . . (*As if *producing trump card*) 'Peter Piper picked a peck of pickled mixed biscuits – mixed biscuits!!!' (*Pause*) That's it then. I'll paint the scenery. NNERRGGGGAA-AAHHHH!!! (*All rush off stage*)

Party Games

EMMA, *glittering hostess at a cocktail party;* ROGER, *her husband, amiable but faintly boorish;* JOANNA, *a fashion-conscious friend of* EMMA'S; CLIVE, *a self-assured dilettante;* JULIAN, *a debonair art historian;* DAVID, *a morose friend of* ROGER'S *and a drag on the party.*

'Party Games' is a satirical sketch, looking at four aspects of behaviour: the first, with the tennis commentary, is the social competitiveness of two women; the second, with the rugby commentary, is intellectual one-upmanship; the third, with the boxing commentary, is the sparring relationship of a husband and wife; and the fourth and most serious, with the cricket commentary, is the social taboo surrounding the subject of death. Each scene takes place with a different combination of characters at a cocktail party. The sketch is really a set piece – perhaps one half of an evening's performance – when performed in its entirety. However, Riding Lights *have frequently performed just the tennis and rugby sequences (as in their revue 'Colour Radio' on the Edinburgh Festival Fringe, 1979) or the tennis, rugby and cricket matches, without the boxing match. More or less any combination will work, though one section does not normally stand on its own. The inclusion of the cricket match may be dictated by the overall emphasis of the evening. Sketches like this, which do not touch on religion directly but explore familiar attitudes, are immensely valuable in a group's repertoire. They appeal to the more sophisticated elements in the audience as well as, hopefully, inspiring a healthy recognition of the evils satirised. However, 'Party Games' needs careful rehearsal and good timing to work well. Directors should feel free to stage the sketch imaginatively without slavishly following these recommendations: The heart of the material is in the handling of the commentaries and we would suggest all the men in unison as tennis umpire,* DAVID *as rugby commentator,* CLIVE *as boxing commentator, and* JULIAN

*as cricket commentator. The choices may depend on the actors'
ability to imitate appropriate TV commentators. Naturally,
additional actors could be used for the commentaries but there
may be dramatic advantages in restricting them to the guests at
the party. If the latter is done, the guests should 'come out of
character' in order to do it and – most important – the other
characters should not be aware of the commentators (in other
words, not look at them or respond to them). As for the verses
after each section, this is a question of taste. If the tennis and
rugby matches are performed alone, then only the verse after
the rugby match should be recited to 'round off' the sketch. If
the whole sketch is done, the verse after the cricket commentary
is essential (and implies at least one other verse being used
earlier). The action of the cocktail party goes on throughout,
but great care should be taken to avoid upstaging the main
focus of action. The way to do this is to arrange the characters
not involved in a sequence to chat silently upstage, with the
minimum of movement.*

EMMA *spruces herself for the arrival of the guests.* ROGER
*wheels on the drinks trolley. The doorbell rings and one by one
the guests arrive :* CLIVE, JULIAN, DAVID. *Improvised greetings
– 'Clive! Long time no see!', 'What can I get you, David?',
'Julian, me old hearty!' General social laughter and pleasantries.
The men chat together, except for* DAVID *who pensively munches
cheese biscuits by the trolley and pours himself the first of
several whiskies.* JOANNA'S *voice is heard offstage : 'Cooee!'
She enters.*

> EMMA : Joanna!
> JOANNA : Emma. Darling!
> EMMA : You sweetie, how super of you to come!
> JOANNA : I could hardly refuse such a fabulous
> invitation card. It's had pride of place
> beside my Louis Quatorze clock.
> UMPIRE : Love fifteen.
> EMMA : Really? I didn't know you had a Louis
> Quatorze clock.

JOANNA: I didn't know you could do such beautiful italic writing, darling. It must have taken you an age to write out every card.

EMMA: They were printed.

UMPIRE: Love thirty.

JOANNA: No! I could have sworn . . . Clive, how are you, and Roger, and Julian, what a pleasant surprise! Emma, you've got together a super crowd of people.

EMMA: It wouldn't have been half so good without you, Joanna, you look fabulous.

JOANNA: Thank you.

EMMA: You can wear absolutely anything and look fabulous. These days I daren't risk anything off the peg, I'd look hideous.

UMPIRE: Fifteen-thirty.

JOANNA: Oh come on, Emma, I don't think you look a day over forty-five.

UMPIRE: Fifteen-forty.

EMMA: I feel it, honey . . . I feel as if I've been dragged through a hedge backwards when I look at you – how on earth do you manage to keep so slim? . . . Talking of slimming, how did the health farm go?

UMPIRE: Thirty-forty.

JOANNA: Fine, darling, thank you.

EMMA: Did the brutes put you on a starvation diet?

JOANNA: Actually, when they saw how I looked, they told me that I didn't need the deep treatment and I was allowed to feed extremely well.

EMMA: (*Removing some succulent pastries*) Well, dear, you won't want to risk one of these on top of all that food – how about a Ritz biscuit?

UMPIRE: Deuce.

JOANNA: It's quite all right, darling, I've just been

told to avoid *real* cream.

UMPIRE: Advantage Mrs. Baxter.

JOANNA: Oh, by the way, I've brought you a bottle of wine. (*She hands it to* EMMA)

EMMA: Darling, how thoughtful . . . Mmmm . . . (*Looking at the label*) You really shouldn't have bothered . . . These Spanish wines are such fantastic value for money, aren't they?

UMPIRE: Deuce.

JOANNA: Yes, they're super.

EMMA: (*Kissing her*) Honey, thank you.

JOANNA: Oh, I forgot, there's a card to go with it – that's for Richard for passing his maths 'A' level.

EMMA: Five pounds . . . Joanna, you shouldn't have . . . Actually, I'm told it was the toughest competition for ten years.

JOANNA: Really? Well, in that case, you must be thankful that he had the experience of the previous three attempts.

UMPIRE: Advantage Mrs. Baxter.

EMMA: Talking about previous attempts, I see you haven't brought that super young chap from Lloyds with you tonight. Is it all off?

UMPIRE: Deuce.

JOANNA: Yes.

EMMA: Pity, I thought he was just your type. Anyway, your husband must be fairly relieved.

UMPIRE: Advantage Mrs. Forsythe.

EMMA: (*Moving over to* JULIAN) You have met Julian, by the way, haven't you?

JOANNA: Well, of course, he won't remember me.

JULIAN: No, I'm afraid I don't.

EMMA: But I was sure you knew each other – the way Joanna spoke about you on the 'phone last week, you sounded like an old friend . . . Now who is everybody going to have – er, *what* is everybody going to have, I should say – Julian, Joanna . . . ?

UMPIRE : Game to Mrs. Forsythe.

ALL : Play up, play up and play the game!
Jolly good show, do as you ought,
Never give up, be a good sport,
Play up, play up and play the game!

ROGER : Talking of ART, Clive, I find a lot of fifteenth century Italian art bores me to death.

CLIVE : Such as?

COMMENTATOR : He's tackled.

ROGER : Well, to be honest with you, Clive, even a lot of the Sistine Chapel ceiling bored me.

COMMENTATOR : But it's out to the fly half.

CLIVE : I'm sorry, I thought you referred to fifteenth century Italian art.

ROGER : Did I? Ah.

COMMENTATOR : Thrown forward. Scrum down.

CLIVE : The Sistine Chapel ceiling was painted 1508–1512, but presumably your guide book told you that when you last visited Rome . . . Actually, when did you last visit Rome, Roger?

COMMENTATOR : He's got possession.

ROGER : Oh . . . It was before the war, of course, I can't remember exactly.

CLIVE : Ah, I understood you were some sort of expert on art.

COMMENTATOR : And it's out down the three-quarter line, going for the corner flag.

ROGER : I wouldn't say expert . . . I just know what I like, you know. I'm a great fan of Leonardo, as a matter of fact.

CLIVE : Which paintings of Leonardo had you in

mind?

COMMENTATOR: Up and under.

ROGER: Well, the *Mona Lisa* for one thing.

CLIVE: And?

ROGER: And many of the others, of course.

CLIVE: Of course.

COMMENTATOR: He's racing down the wing.

ROGER: What about yourself?

COMMENTATOR: But a beautiful bodycheck from the full-back.

CLIVE: Me? Oh, I didn't say I was a fan of Leonardo.

COMMENTATOR: Knocked on. Scrum down.

CLIVE: No, I'm very partial to the later extravagances of Giulio Romano.

COMMENTATOR: A dramatic break down the three-quarter line.

CLIVE: Mannerism has a perverse sort of appeal to me.

COMMENTATOR: Lovely dummy scissors.

ROGER: What is Mannerism, exactly?

COMMENTATOR: Look at that high tackle!

CLIVE: Mannerism . . . well . . . it's a period in Italian isn't it, Roger . . . about the time of Michelangelo . . .

COMMENTATOR: He's struggling on, about twenty yards to go.

ROGER: I mean, who are the Mannerist painters, other than Giulio Romano?

CLIVE: Um . . . aah . . .

COMMENTATOR: No, he's down and the ball's knocked into touch. Line out.

ROGER: Ah well, I thought you were supposed to be our brilliant art expert.

COMMENTATOR: Not straight, a penalty kick. And now look at the concentration as he takes that kick.

CLIVE: Bronzino's *Cupid and Psyche* in the

National Gallery, of course, is a fairly
good example of Mannerist painting.

COMMENTATOR: And what a kick!

CLIVE: I find Parmigianino somewhat extrava-
gant, but then Pope-Hennessy's discussion of Michelangelo's *Last Judgement*
explains a great deal of familiar Mannerist motifs.

COMMENTATOR: It's a try, it's a try, what a text book try;
straight through those defence lines like
a knife through butter.

ROGER: You studied art, did you?

CLIVE: No, I'm a civil engineer, actually.

COMMENTATOR: What studied coolness as he prepares for
the place kick.

ROGER: Well, I've got to hand it to you, Clive, you
know quite a bit about art on the quiet.

COMMENTATOR: Look at that ball sail straight over the bar
and between the posts.

ROGER: I know who to get my information from
about Mannerism!

COMMENTATOR: A perfect conversion. (JULIAN *walks over
to* CLIVE)

JULIAN: I've been thinking – haven't we met
before?

COMMENTATOR: Just a few more minutes of injury time.

CLIVE: No, I don't think we have.

JULIAN: I'm sure I saw you this morning flipping
through one of my catalogues on the
Mannerist exhibition at the National
Gallery.

COMMENTATOR: He's in trouble.

CLIVE: Er, you wrote the catalogue on the
Mannerist exhibition?

JULIAN: That's right.

ROGER: Well, if you're interested in Mannerism,
you should talk to Clive, he knows all
about it.

CLIVE: Er, well . . .

COMMENTATOR: The forwards are just piling into that loose ruck . . . He's in really serious trouble.

ROGER: Clive could knock anybody into a cocked hat when it comes to Mannerism – one of the most knowledgeable people in the country.

JULIAN: Really? It's strange I haven't heard about you.

COMMENTATOR: Scrum five and they're going for the shove over.

CLIVE: (*Fumbling for a distraction*) Um . . . (*Seeing* DAVID *pouring himself another whisky*) Joanna, you've been very quiet this evening!

COMMENTATOR: It's out to the fly-half.

CLIVE: Have you met this fellow Julian?

COMMENTATOR: He's kicked for touch. And it's all over, and what a nail-biting performance it was.

ALL: Play up, play up and play the game!
The object is to keep your cool,
And make your neighbour feel a fool,
Play up, play up and play the game!
(*They all raise their glasses*) Cheers!
(*Hubbub of conversation*)

EMMA: Now, what would everybody like to drink? Clive?

CLIVE: A gin-and-it wouldn't go down amiss, thanks.

EMMA: Super. Roger, can you organise a gin-and-it for Clive? (EMMA *and* ROGER *exchange comments, heard only by the* COMMENTATOR, *as they move around the room, talk to the guests and offer drinks*)

ROGER: We're right out of gin.

EMMA: But I put it on the list.

ROGER : The off-licence was closed.

EMMA : You mean, you forgot to go to the off-licence.

ROGER : Are you saying I'm a liar?

EMMA : That's for you to decide, honey.

COMMENTATOR : And in the red corner it's Mrs. Forsythe, and in the blue corner it's Mr. Forsythe.

EMMA : And another thing, our bedroom looked like a bomb had hit it at six o'clock. You know perfectly well I use it for people's coats.

COMMENTATOR : A swift punch to the chest.

EMMA : Julian, is everything shipshape?

JULIAN : Yes, I'm working my way through these cheese biscuits, they're really divine.

EMMA : That's fabulous, darling. (*To* ROGER) I suppose it was too much to ask that you might have done something for a change, like clear it up?

COMMENTATOR : He's got to watch that stinging right-hander.

EMMA : Joanna, can I get you a refill?

JOANNA : That's terribly sweet of you, I'd love one.

EMMA : (*To* ROGER, *who is picking up a vol-au-vent from the table*) Don't stand there stuffing yourself, get out and talk to people.

COMMENTATOR : She's running rings round him.

ROGER : They're your friends, I don't see why I should talk to them.

COMMENTATOR : He's ducking out of trouble.

EMMA : I don't have to remind you that it was your idea to have this party? But, of course, if I hadn't sent out the invitations nobody would ever have got one.

ROGER : Well, I . . .

COMMENTATOR : She's caught him on the wrong foot.

EMMA : (*Between her teeth, as she smiles at* CLIVE) You're utterly selfish, Roger.

COMMENTATOR: He's taking a lot of punishment.

EMMA: Clive, I'm so thrilled you could come, now what will you have?

CLIVE: Well, I'm rather partial to these, actually.

EMMA: Good, so long as you're enjoying yourself, that's super. (*She sweeps past* ROGER)

ROGER: I suppose you think you're Coco Chanel or somebody, do you – wafting all over the place?

COMMENTATOR: A borderline low punch, there.

ROGER: Well, let me tell you, you're making an ass of yourself at this party.

COMMENTATOR: A dramatic come-back, he's obviously intending to go the full distance.

EMMA: Joanna, I must introduce you to Clive, he's absolutely fascinating.

JOANNA: I've been dying to meet him.

EMMA: You'll get on terrifically well. (*To* ROGER) The only ass in this house is you, standing around making a total fool of yourself, tossing off wildly inaccurate statements about subjects you know nothing about.

COMMENTATOR: But she's right back in there, pummelling away his resistance.

EMMA: Couldn't you see that Clive was vastly more intelligent than you?

COMMENTATOR: She's going for the early knockout.

EMMA: No, you couldn't. You're probably slewed out of your mind.

COMMENTATOR: The whiplash blow to the forehead.

EMMA: When I meet people like Clive and Julian, I sometimes wonder why I married you.

COMMENTATOR: He's out for the count.

ROGER: Do you regret marrying me?

COMMENTATOR: One, two . . .

EMMA: Frankly, yes.

COMMENTATOR: Four, five, six . . .

EMMA: If it wasn't for the children –

COMMENTATOR: Eight, nine . . .

EMMA: I would have left you years ago.

COMMENTATOR: Ten. He's out.

EMMA: Julian, can I possibly tempt you to one of these banana boats?

JULIAN: Emma, it's really very good of you and Roger to do all this, you know.

EMMA: Oh, the pleasure is ours, we absolutely revel in it.

ALL: (*With conspicuously less panache than before, they raise their glasses*)
Play up, play up and play the game!
Never tiring, never sagging,
Keeping on, though spirits flagging,
Play up, play up and play the game!
Cheers . . .

EMMA: Now, David, how are you managing? You've been frightfully quiet this evening.

DAVID: I've been feeling a little down, actually . . . the wife . . . you know how it is . . .

EMMA: How is she, the poor thing?

DAVID: Not . . . um . . . not too good, you know how it is.

COMMENTATOR: She's getting a lot of movement off the pitch, but he's not going to take any chances with this attacking field.

CLIVE: Cheer up, old chap, she'll pull through all right – see if she doesn't!

COMMENTATOR: Bowled him a googly there.

DAVID: Thanks Clive, but I don't think she will this time, the doctor says . . . It's a matter of time, really.

COMMENTATOR: But he's hooked it to the boundary.

EMMA: I must send her some flowers.

DAVID: It's kind of you, Emma, but she's not conscious, so she won't appreciate them.

COMMENTATOR: Bowled him a little wide there.

JOANNA: Could I take the children for a few days? I could take them off to the country, down to Lulworth Cove – it's so beautiful. I've got a cottage near there. Do you know Dorset, Clive? I think the south coast is fabulous at this time of year.

COMMENTATOR: Clive comes in past umpire Buller.

CLIVE: Yes, actually, I often have holidays on the Isle of Wight.

JOANNA: Really?

DAVID: The trouble is what to do with the children in a few months time.

COMMENTATOR: Nearly caught him in the gulley there, but he's digging himself in.

DAVID: You know, I keep wondering what to do when –

EMMA: Would everyone like some coffee?

DAVID: When it's all over . . . after . . . after Amanda's –

EMMA: Now, David, will you have some coffee?

COMMENTATOR: She's making him fish round outside the off stump.

DAVID: I mean, after Amanda is dead.

COMMENTATOR: But he's hooked it for six!

CLIVE: Good heavens, look at the time!

ALL: 'OWZAT!'

DAVID: It's only half-past nine.

CLIVE: So it is.

COMMENTATOR: He's dropped the catch.

DAVID: Dead. I can hardly believe it. Dead . . .

EMMA: Coffee, coffee!

DAVID: Do you think death is the end, Roger?

COMMENTATOR: A fast single down to third man.

ROGER: Oh, I've been near to it many times in the war, you know . . . funny thing war . . . Actually, I was in the Royal West Kent Regiment for a short spell – time of my life. Shan't forget that in a hurry.

COMMENTATOR : Wide.

DAVID : I keep asking myself, what's the point of all this? I mean, it's not just the fact that Amanda is going to die, it's just the thought that we'll all be dead in –

EMMA : David, isn't it hospital visiting time? We shan't mind a bit if you have to nip off.

COMMENTATOR : A beautifully flighted off-break.

DAVID : Actually, she's in the intensive care unit, I wouldn't be any help. No, it's the thought that death comes to us all . . .

CLIVE : Did you know that you can have four men standing on an ostrich egg without breaking it?

ROGER : Good heavens.

EMMA : I can't believe it.

CLIVE : No, really.

ALL : 'OWZAT!'

COMMENTATOR : No ball.

DAVID : Dead . . . Do you know what that means? This body, this magnificent instrument, reduced to a shell.

ROGER : Look, for heaven's sake, old chap – don't go on and on.

EMMA : You've got overtired, we all understand. I've got your things here – and I honestly think that you'd benefit from a good night's sleep. Here's your coat.

ALL : 'OWZAT!'

COMMENTATOR : She's bowled him. Bowled him middle stump and he goes away towards the pavilion, shaking his head.

DAVID : But I keep thinking – any of us could die tomorrow, we could die in our beds tonight!

CLIVE : Look here, think of the ladies, David.

DAVID : Joanna, *do* you think death is the end?

JOANNA : I think . . . I think I'd like another drink.

DAVID: I could go out in my car now, any of us
could go out in our cars now, straight
down the main road and crash into a
lampost.

EMMA: David, please.

CLIVE: This is hardly cricket, old chap.

DAVID: Suddenly, that's it . . . shutters . . . wham
. . . that's it.

ROGER: What you need is a good, stiff drink. Here
now, play the game, David. Drinks all
round, Emma, Joanna, Clive, Julian.

ALL: Play up, play up and play the game!
We'll play it to our final breath
And never, ever mention d –
Play up, play up and play the game!

CREATING LAUGHTER

If you tried to describe a colour to someone who is colourblind, or to explain the phenomenon of snow to a nomad in the desert, it would be easier than explaining a joke to someone who has no sense of humour. For laughter, by its nature, resists analysis. It is unpredictable, sudden, elusive, sometimes cruel and frequently absurd.

Perhaps this 'irrational' element in laughter prompts the observations of men like St. John Chrysostom, that though the gospels record the tears of Christ there is no suggestion that he ever laughed, or explains the fear of flippancy which lies behind the words of the Preacher: 'Sorrow is better than laughter; for by the sadness of the countenance the heart is made better.' (Ecclesiastes 7 v. 3). But are tears the only approach to God? Men, women and, above all, children laugh the world over. Some of the greatest Christians have been characterised by their ability to laugh at themselves and have rejoiced in a profound sense of humour. Numerous stories from the Bible and the experience of countless individuals show that God has given the gift of laughter as a reflection of his own eternal character. (See 'God and Humour', *Time to Act*, p. 120.) If, then, we are to communicate the warmth and love of Christ, the joy and sincere humanity of the gospels, this cannot be achieved artistically without creating laughter as a vital ingredient of the message. But there are many kinds of laughter and many ways of creating laughter. A sensitive and discriminating approach is necessary for the Christian, as well as sound artistic judgement. Actors and writers concerned to explore this potential need to understand the elements of comedy, then to master the art of performance and finally to command the responsiveness of an audience. There is no substitute for experience, or for natural talent, and no limit to development – great performers find a lifetime too short

to learn the art. Nevertheless, the following observations
are intended to be an encouragement to learn from practice,
rather than theory.

The elements of comedy

Incongruity: This is when something seems 'out of place' or
does not normally relate to the other elements in the story.
The Bible is full of examples – so much so, that one could
claim that God's familiar means of communication to man
is essentially comic: for instance, childbirth and extreme
old age (Abraham and Sarah), an ass talking to a prophet
(Balaam), the youngest member of the smallest family of the
least important tribe of Israel chosen to defeat the Midianites
(Gideon), local shepherds in Bethlehem receiving the
greatest visionary experience in history, the prodigal son
given a lavish party (the parables of Jesus), a condemned
criminal promised eternal life in paradise. Although there
is much more than humour in these incidents (and in many
cases great dramatic intensity) the awareness of incongruity
as an expression of God's condescending love makes them
essentially joyful. They contain the seeds of laughter. Most
comic situations in the theatre depend on incongruity in
some form or another, and careful observation of life, as
well as a close understanding of the Bible, will furnish many
examples.

Surprise: The best humour is frequently unpredictable – a
door opens and a character appears who is supposed to be
somewhere else; a stranger reveals her true identity; or – in
the gospels – two disciples find they have been discussing
the events of the passion with the risen Christ himself (the
road to Emmaus). When the audience is genuinely surprised,
or watches a character on stage being surprised by events,
this will produce either laughter or dramatic tension,
according to the context. Surprise of both kinds – audience
and actors – is a crucial element in good writing, acting or
directing, and is fundamental to theatre of all kinds.

Wordplay: This is one of the oldest elements of comedy and – when well exploited – delights the audience with revelations of double-meanings. The obvious form of this is the pun, and the Bible contains quite a number. Jeremiah, for instance, sees a rod of almond as a sign that God is watching over Israel but the Hebrew word used for the 'rod' and for 'watching' are practically identical, forming a memorable pun. Puns in excess can be very tiresome (notably in the youthful Shakespeare) but a great deal of contemporary humour – especially the 'Goons' – is rooted in puns and double-meaning.

Reversals: When expectations are reversed, people will often laugh. For example, a famous epitaph reads: 'Here lies the body of Major James Brush, who was killed by the accidental discharge of a pistol by his orderly, 8th April, 1814. "Well done, good and faithful servant."' This is a total reversal of the accepted notion of a servant. Another reversal, inherently comic, is contained in the account of the blind man healed by Christ (John 9). His directness to the pharisees and dogged conviction of his own healing put this beggar in a position of authority over the doctors of the law and they resent the implied reversal: 'You were born in utter sin and would you teach us?' Although this could be dramatised quite seriously, the character of the blind man and the naked irony of the story suggest strong comic potential (which does not preclude an overall seriousness of intention).

Deflation: This is one of the richest elements of comedy. A serious dramatic production is often vulnerable to accidental deflation, as when the heroine in *Tosca* flung herself from a tower in a suicidal leap, supposedly to land on a mattress out of sight of the audience, but was so heavy that she bounced up over a wall in full view of the auditorium. The net result was five minutes hysterical laughter from an audience supposed to be witnessing a great operatic tragedy. 'Deflation', when used as a deliberate comic device, can function as a guardian of common sense. It can show pompousness to be ridiculous, or uncontrolled anger to be essentially absurd. One character can deflate the comments of another (see Ananias and Flora in 'A Funny Thing') or circumstances can show the folly of pretentiousness (see the fate of Goliath in 'David and Goliath'). In our own century, many forms of extremism – from religious bigotry to National Socialism in Germany – have been characterised by petty tyrants taking themselves intensely seriously. Humour in all its forms, from slapstick to mimicry to satire, can expose the ludicrous nature of such illusions and safeguard societies from fanaticism. It is such a powerful weapon that it needs careful aim, but it is fair to say that the true spirit of Christianity, characterised by joy, humility and self-sacrifice, has little to fear from deflation, whereas the lies of the devil are the most vulnerable target. Hell, it might be added, is a place where there is no sense of humour. *Recognition:* This is when we see ourselves clearly mirrored in the comedy or recognise the accuracy of an observation. Mimics depend totally on this element in comedy, but in a broader sense it should be true of the characters and situations that we see on stage. For this reason, an audience will laugh more when they can relate to what is happening (children, for instance, will miss jokes about politics, whereas adults may well miss jokes about the 'bionic man'). If an audience recognise a 'type', or a certain kind of 'jargon', or a particular attitude, this will give the comedy greater plausibility and the response will be correspondingly enthusiastic (see section below on 'commanding an audience'). Comedy goes wrong most frequently when there is no point of contact.

The art of performing comedy

Timing: This is learnt by experience. In most cases an actor should have silence and stillness for delivering a comic line, but it should never be delivered too late. If the lines come too slowly, a scene begins to become 'soggy', the pace slows up, and the audience becomes strained. A line delivered too fast, however, can sometimes be lost in the laughter over a previous line, or 'upstaged' by somebody else's movement. It cannot be emphasised too strongly that the instinct for timing and the acquiring of great sensitivity to audiences and other actors is the essence of comic performance.

Underplaying: 'Overplaying' comic situations is a disaster area for amateur productions but, judging by the average television comedy and more than a few repertory and West End productions, the pitfalls are just as deadly to the professional actor. If an actor gives too much emphasis to a comic line, or smiles at his own witticisms, or laughs at other situations on stage, he may well kill the humour. It is impossible to analyse this without looking at each situation in turn but – generally speaking – a 'deadpan' approach to comedy is often the best. This is particularly true when the comedy is satirical and depends on the characters taking themselves seriously. In the case of obvious witticisms (when the character will know that he is being funny) it is often better to 'throw away' the line than say it with too much aplomb. This, however, needs skill – for the line must be perfectly timed, well heard by the audience and yet delivered as if it were a casual observation just thought up by the character (not laboriously constructed by a writer and then carefully rehearsed for three weeks). The tradition of pantomime, when characters frequently deliver their lines with great emphasis straight out to the audience encourages damaging habits for the aspiring comedy actor. It is better to be as plausible and as natural as possible.

Characterisation: Much of the best comedy is produced by the convincing characterisation of a part – the way an actor walks, gestures, his mannerisms and inflections. Some actors develop this to such a fine art that audiences will laugh at 'who they are' rather than 'what they say'. Writers who create strong comic characters, and actors who live up to this challenge, will produce much more powerful comedy than is possible with a series of funny lines. Some playwrights, who are naturally witty, are often tempted to give all their characters the same gift of repartee – they cannot resist a funny line when they think of one. But a more subtle approach is to carefully study the drama from life, providing each character with a consistent language and appropriate reactions to each situation, above all allowing for the creation of unconscious humour when people take themselves too seriously. (In this case, it will often be the way a character misses the point, or fails to say something, that will be funnier than a conscious witticism.) In exactly the same way, an actor needs acute observation and strict self-discipline in the creation of a comic role. A mannerism, like a silly laugh for instance, can be very infectious, but over-used will alienate an audience. The actor should create entirely believable, subtle portraits of human beings, avoiding clichés such as professors who wander round clutching their lapels or telephone receptionists who continuously manicure their nails. Accurate observations of genuine idiosyncracies of behaviour lie behind the most memorable comic performances.

Expression: There are many ways of saying a line, and many modes of expressing joy, frustration, anger, hope. A supple use of the face, well characterised gestures and voice control all add the vital element of credibility to comedy. Essentially part of characterisation, expression depends on accurate observation of how people react: a subtle performer will know how to say a line like 'Well, that's super, isn't it?' to imply, 'That's a complete disaster.' Technically, this may mean saying it too strongly, or saying the line absolutely expressionlessly, or letting the audience see some frustrated gesture (like screwing up a paper serviette) which goes in the opposite direction to the surface meaning of the line. Good facial expressions will often make an audience laugh in anticipation of a line or a situation – always a sign that the comedy is working well.

Staging: An actor must always be positioned for maximum impact. In other words, he must not be upstaged if he is the central focus of the comedy. This does not mean he has to be downstage with all the other actors upstage, but it does mean that the audience's attention should be focused on him. Sometimes, it can add to the humour when an actor delivers a line from an unexpected position (under the bed etc.). The important thing is for the director to avoid any visual distractions at the crucial moment.

Commanding an audience

This is the greatest challenge of all to the comedy actor. Even though every aspect of the performance is good, if the audience are not 'won over' the comedy will fall flat. The mood of an audience is a mysterious phenomenon. Audiences can vary in reaction enormously from one night to another – they cannot be made to laugh against their will (some just appear to lack vitality) but it is usually up to the cast to create the right atmosphere and, when this is achieved, an audience will respond gladly.

Seating arrangement: Audiences that are small and scattered round a large hall, often at too great a distance from the stage, will respond sluggishly. They should be seated close together, in reasonable warmth, and – ideally – suitable music should be played before a performance to create atmosphere and a sense of expectation. Obviously, if a sketch is performed during a service, the actors will inherit the mood of the previous half hour or so and care should be paid to the manner of the introduction and choice of the sketch. Congregations are a complex form of audience (especially when they contain elements that have not been expecting drama) and should be treated with great sensitivity – and never jolted too abruptly from a reflective to hilarious mood.

Punctual start: An audience that has been kept waiting for too long may be difficult to handle; a few minutes grace for latecomers should be quite sufficient.

Contact: The clue to handling an audience is to understand that it has a personality of its own. This is sometimes dominated by a few people who may laugh at certain kinds of things more than others, but – despite the different elements – audiences tend to react as one. The secret, therefore, is to make contact with the prevalent mood in the audience – to appeal to the particular audience, to make friends. Audiences, like people, need to feel included; if they feel 'out of a joke' – or feel that the actors don't like them – the members of an audience will be inhibited. Affection is at the heart of good comedy. This implies a mutual response – the actors give and the audience gives back; as the actors give more to the audience and the audience becomes more susceptible to their charms, the audience laughs more readily and more infectiously as the performance develops.

It would be a fair summary of this article to say that a shared sense of humour is an expression of love, and the greater the love between the actors and the audience, the richer will be the comedy.

A NOTE ON SATIRE

The word 'satire' was introduced into the English language around the beginning of the sixteenth century, or a little before. During the Renaissance people rediscovered a penchant for classical literature and there they discovered that 'satura' was popular in ancient times. 'Satura' – literally a medley – was originally a verse satire in which prevailing vices and follies were held up to ridicule. One writer, Quintillian, claimed that the Romans thought of it first. Satire is, of course, no longer confined to poems; satiric prose was common in the eighteenth century and there has been much written for the theatre which could be called satirical. However, the purpose of this article is not to discuss literary evolution but rather to consider the nature of satire and its usefulness to the Christian writer.

How does it work?

As a literary means of denouncing, exposing or deriding folly, satire achieves this, in general, through a comic method. The devices of ridicule and exaggeration, distortion and caricature are often employed, even though the satire itself may have been initially provoked by a deep sense of moral outrage. Satire is a very practical form of writing and because it is political or social or moral in its objectives, it requires a wide readership. For satire to work, it relies on finding agreement with a significant proportion of its readership, whose laughter and enjoyment of the satire will shame those who are on the receiving end into renouncing the folly or vice in question. Occasionally, the horror of public exposure or the standing of the satirist will be sufficient to bring about the desired change, but usually widespread agreement expressed in laughter is necessary.

To agree, presupposes sharing the same moral platform from which the satirist has launched his attack, since he can only be successful by appealing to a common standard of reasonableness, decent behaviour, wisdom, morality, virtue or common sense. That commonly respected moral platform is non-existent in our modern society, so there is little effective satire and what there is has little chance of appealing to a wide audience. What we often see today is an anarchistic kind of satire, where *everything* is made ridiculous (except the position of the satirist, of course); moral understanding has largely been eaten away, so little can be 'exposed'. Instead of pointing out the ridiculous *within* things, the ridiculous is overlaid *onto* them. The exercise becomes surreal or purposeless – the only objective being laughter itself, which is true of farce rather than satire. Some modern satirists have complained that, 'There aren't any sacred cows left.' That may well have been correct, but, of course, the one sacred cow left to be satirised is the position of the satirists themselves, the island of their own self-esteem and the folly of living in a world where nothing is sacred.

What are the dangers?

The main danger for the satirist is *arrogance*. By using his skill to pull down to size or to expose, he must pass judgement on other people and their actions, but if he uses his power to put himself on a pedestal, then he, too, must be pulled down. One way for the writer to avoid this danger is to base his satire on an authority higher than himself. Another danger for the writer is to see satire as a *weapon* with which to inflict as much damage as possible. An angry man holding a weapon can lose his head and turn a piece which sets out to be corrective, into something which is downright malicious. If the satire is too coarse (too exaggerated, too distorted, too absurd) it will risk missing its mark. Effective satire is often sharp but also subtle.

Some cartoonists, for instance, are so vicious that their caricatures not only suggest that, for example, a particular politician is a corrupt monster, but also that the imagination of the artist himself is warped. Reactions which are over-extreme discredit themselves. On the other hand, satire may also miss its target by allowing the humour to cloud the 'serious' issue, instead of revealing it. Finally, there is the danger of *mockery*. Whereas satire arises from the feeling that something important is at stake, and should imply a concern for the best interests of the people involved and the issues raised, mockery does none of these things.

Satire and the Christian writer

A Christian writer should, first of all, be alive to the dangers outlined above, but then he should carefully assess the likely response to his satire, particularly over issues where his authority is most liable to be questioned. In these instances satire may not be the wisest approach. Although the Christian is strongly warned against making spiritual judgements about his fellow human beings on his own authority, at the same time he is called to be salt in the world, to fight evil, to encourage others in wisdom and maturity and to share his understanding of truth; this can only be done on the authority of God, otherwise it would be presumptuous. It is also interesting that all these aspects of a Christian's calling correspond closely with satire; the one difference appears to be the issue of laughter, and making things look ridiculous. Does God give us the authority to do that? The answer given by the Bible is 'yes'. Apart from the many instances of satirical teaching spread throughout the Bible (e.g. about the Fool or the Sluggard in Proverbs), we are told clearly on several occasions that 'God scorns the wicked . . . He who sits in the heavens laughs; the Lord has them in derision . . . The Lord laughs at the wicked, for He sees that His day is coming.' At times, God's attitude to man's sinful folly appears to be satirical.

There is a penetrating and very funny piece of satire in Isaiah 44. In a general way, over several chapters, Isaiah is expressing God's feelings about the idolatry that the Israelites have fallen into while they have been in exile in Babylon. This crystallises in a sustained piece of satire in verses 9–20 of chapter 44, in which the absurdity of worshipping blocks of wood is spelt out. In order to get through to the exiles, the prophet needed a strong, rational approach, coloured with humour, which would knock the 'status quo' of stupid idol-worship. The result is effective.

It is clear, then, that God's Word endorses the use of satire; the Christian writer must be equally clear that God would endorse his *motives*. God's attitude to mankind is characterised by unending compassionate love; he disciplines waywardness also out of love and he urges us to speak the truth only in love. This was the way Jesus corrected people and was his underlying motive even when he was lashing the hypocrisy of the Pharisees with stern invective. Love did not prevent him from using strong words; it gave him a reason to use them. As Jonathan Swift wrote about himself,

> *Yet malice never was his aim,*
> *He lashed the vice, but spared the name.*

The Christian satirist has a very important role to fulfil but he will only be successful if he tries to understand the feelings of God, if he expresses himself with sharpness, wit and good humour, and if he always retains a sense of his own weakness and a healthy attitude to his own foibles. Swift also said,

> *Satire is a sort of glass, wherein beholders do generally discover everybody's face but their own.*

A Christian writer should try and put that right and have regular inspections of his own face.

(For further development of this subject, 'Party Games' (p. 61) and 'Spreading the Word Around a Bit' (p. 97) are worth reading.)

HOME TRUTHS

Performing sketches is not merely a way of communicating to others. Perhaps the primary value lies in exposing the truth about ourselves. Some of these sketches, like 'David and Goliath' with its simple message of trust, are suitable for any context, but others will find their mark particularly in a Christian context. 'Faithful are the wounds of a friend' might be the motto for a drama group speaking to their own church about gossip or hypocrisy, but there is an equal need to adopt the motto 'Lift up your hearts'. Encouragement through drama can be a way of bringing God's word to a church.

David and Goliath

NARRATOR; CHORUS (*anything from five to fifteen actors*)

This is a highly theatrical piece, requiring great energy and strong chorus interaction, which is difficult to convey fully in print. The sketch is built round the rhythm of an army on the march and was originally written for a children's service, though it works extremely well for audiences of all ages. The use of group narration, strong rhythm, sound effects and stylised action is an exciting combination and could be adapted for many other stories. It is a very reliable style, particularly for street theatre.

The sketch is performed by the CHORUS, *of which the* NARRATOR *is the leader, and from which other, individual characters emerge as required.* 'RHYTHM' *indicates the sound of marching made by the chorus slapping their thighs and this keeps strictly to a repeated four-beat sequence –* dadaDUM DUM DUM DUM, dadaDUM DUM DUM DUM *etc; or musically (♫‖: ♩ ♩ ♩ ♫:‖).* 'FX' *is shorthand for appropriate verbal sound effects. The giant* GOLIATH *can be made by draping a step-ladder with a cloth; an actor, wearing a helmet and huge rubber hands stands on the ladder in such a way that only his head is visible above the cloth. An addition to this could be two other actors standing behind the cloth, each playing a leg and an arm, which they swing alternately in time to the rhythm. The sketch begins with the rhythm, started by the* NARRATOR, *picked up by the* CHORUS, *then fading away into the distance.*

> NARRATOR: In the days when men fought like animals.
> CHORUS: (*FX Different animal noises*)
> NARRATOR: And died like gnats.
> CHORUS: (*FX VVZZZZZ Splat*)
> NARRATOR: Men banded themselves together into great armies to teach each other a thing

or two.

CHORUS: (*Rhythm*)

NARRATOR: Pillaging, ravaging, skirmishing, scavenging.

CHORUS: Pillaging, ravaging, skirmishing, scavenging.

NARRATOR: Now one day, (*Rhythm stops*) King Saul of Israel was in his palace, eating his lunch.

CHORUS: (*With action*) Munch, munch, lovely lunch, munch, munch, lovely lunch, munch, munch.

NARRATOR: When news arrived.

CHORUS: (*FX Choking on lunch*) Whassat!??

NARRATOR The Philistines are coming!

CHORUS: Oh, No! The Philistines are coming! (*Rhythm*)

NARRATOR: Now, in terms of fighting after lunch,
The Philistines were an ugly bunch.
They were the biggest in the land,
And Israelites they couldn't stand.
The Philistines got nearer and nearer and bigger and bigger. (*Rhythm louder*) The Israelites got smaller and smaller and paler and paler. (*Rhythm softer*) They shot their arrows.

CHORUS: (*FX Action firing two arrows*)

NARRATOR: But the arrows just bounced off the Philistines.

CHORUS: (*FX Arrows bouncing off armour*)

NARRATOR: So they threw their spears.

CHORUS: (*FX, Action hurling spears*)

NARRATOR: But the spears just bounced off the Philistines.

CHORUS: (*FX Larger metal objects hitting armour. Rhythm*)

NARRATOR: And the Philistines stopped. 'Halt!'

CHORUS: Dadumpf!

NARRATOR: And the Israelites stopped. (*Quavering*) 'Halt!'

CHORUS: Dadumpf!

NARRATOR: And they glared at each other across the valley.

CHORUS: GLARE! GLARE!

NARRATOR: (*During this speech*, GOLIATH *sets himself*) Now, the Philistines had a sensational secret weapon. It was a man called Goliath, who was ten feet tall. Goliath was big for his age. You know the kind of guy who'd kick sand in your face at the seaside? Well, Goliath was the kind of guy who'd kick whole *beaches* in your face. And he had a horrible laugh.

CHORUS: (*Sonorously*) Huh, huh, huh, huh, HA, HA, AAAHH!

NARRATOR: Every day, they gave him a barn full of whole-wheat nourishment.

CHORUS: (*FX, Action. One actor pitchforks two bales of food into* GOLIATH'S *mouth. Noisy eating*)

NARRATOR: Then he would march up and down the valley,

CHORUS: (*Rhythm.* GOLIATH *begins to march on the spot*)

NARRATOR: Shouting . . .

CHORUS: Come and fight me, come and fight me, scaredicats, scaredicats, nyeah, nyeah, nyeah. (*Repeat*)

NARRATOR: And in the silence, you could hear the Israelites hearts beating.

CHORUS: (*FX, Action baBOM, baBOM, baBOM*)

NARRATOR: No one would take up the challenge.

VOICE 1: Er, 'fraid not . . . bit too close to breakfast for me, old chap. Rice Krispies bobbing up and down, so er . . .

VOICE 2: Sorry. Gammy leg.

VOICE 3: I'm playing squash in half an hour, so I

                    couldn't possibly . . .
NARRATOR : But Goliath continued to march up and
                    down the valley.
  CHORUS : (*Rhythm*)
NARRATOR : Shouting . . .
  CHORUS : Come and fight me, come and fight me,
                    scaredi . . .
     DAVID : I'll fight you! (*He stands in front of group*)
  VOICE 1 : Who said that?
     DAVID : I did.
  VOICE 2 : Where are you?
     DAVID : Here.
NARRATOR : Where?
     DAVID : HERE.
  CHORUS : (*Derisive laughter*)
NARRATOR : It was David.
  VOICE 3 : Come off it. He's only someone's baby
                    brother.
NARRATOR : But David was determined to go and
                    fight Goliath.
  CHORUS : (*Rhythm.* DAVID *picks this up with his feet*)
NARRATOR : He refused all the armour they offered
                    him and trusted in God alone. He took
                    his sling and five smooth stones. (DAVID
                    collects them)
  CHORUS : One, two, three, four, five. (*Rhythm*)
NARRATOR : When Goliath saw David coming to-
                    wards him, he laughed his horrible laugh.
  CHORUS : Huh, huh, huh, huh, HA, HA, AAAHH!
NARRATOR : And shouted –
  GOLIATH : I'll pulverise yer, yer little squirt!
     DAVID : I may be little, but God's on my side!
  GOLIATH : SHUDDUUUPP!!
  CHORUS : (*Rhythm*)
NARRATOR : So David took his sling, put a stone in it
                    and FIRED.
  CHORUS : (*FX, Action, whirling sling four times*)
     DAVID : Catch this one, Goliath.

CHORUS: (*FX Stone hitting forehead*)

NARRATOR: And Goliath caught it – right between the eyes and crashed to the ground.

CHORUS: (*Cheering*)

NARRATOR: And when the Israelites saw that Goliath was dead and that God was on their side, they took heart.

VOICE 1: Oh, I say! Jolly good show!

VOICE 2: Wizard prang!

VOICE 3: Spiffing!

VOICE 4: Really wopped him there, David.

VOICE 5: Cracking fine shot!

NARRATOR: And the Israelites charged. 'Tally-ho!'

CHORUS: (*Sing opening bars of 'Willian Tell Overture'. Disintegrates into battle noise*)

NARRATOR: And the Philistines fled in panic.

CHORUS: (*FX Screams and pattering feet into distance*)

NARRATOR: So they shot their arrows after them.

CHORUS: (*FX Firing two arrows*)

NARRATOR: And they were all killed, to the last man.

VOICE 1: 'ERE, 'ang about. *I'm* the last man.

CHORUS: (*All fire arrows at him*)

VOICE 1: (*Sudden, St. Sebastian-style death*)

CHORUS: (*Rhythm*)

NARRATOR: Why did David defeat Goliath? (*Someone raises hand*) Yes?

VOICE 2: Because he trusted in God.

NARRATOR: (*As Israelite*) So he did.

CHORUS: (*Severally*) 'By Jove, that's a good scheme.' 'Just the ticket', 'Should have tried that one before', 'I'll say'.

VOICE 3: Well, what about having a crack at it now?

NARRATOR: Why not?

CHORUS: (*With rhythm and words fading to silence*) Trust in God, trust in God, trust in God . . .

An Eye for an Eye

NARRATOR ONE; NARRATOR TWO; MR. FANG, *a dentist, who also plays* CHARACTER A; MR. SQUINT, *an optician, who also plays* CHARACTER B; A JUDGE

This format, two narrators plus accompanying mime, is well-tried and is very reliable in buildings which are large enough to necessitate the use of a PA system. The 'ping-pong' nature of the dialogue gives the sketch a secure structure which has pace and liveliness. This sketch is also interesting in that it is based on a passage from the Sermon on the Mount that, at first sight, might look rather undramatic.

The scene opens in a courtroom. The two narrators are dressed as barristers; they stand downstage left and right, respectively. Messrs. FANG *and* SQUINT *are seated upstage centre, on either side of the* JUDGE'S *chair.* FANG *is wearing an eyepatch;* SQUINT'S *jaw is heavily bandaged. They both rise as the* JUDGE *enters. All three sit down.*

> ONE: Silence in court.
> TWO: Silence!
> ONE: (*As* JUDGE) Proceed.
> TWO: Mr. Fang, the dentist . . .
> ONE: Your Honour.
> TWO: Is hereby accused . . .
> ONE: Of disfiguring the smile of Mr. Squint, the optician . . .
> TWO: By the unnecessary removal . . .
> ONE: Of a prominent tooth.
> TWO: Justice, m'lud, justice!
> ONE: (*As* JUDGE) Let justice be done.
> TWO: Mr. Squint. (SQUINT *steps forward with size eight tongs and removes tooth from* FANG)

ONE: Objection, m'lud.

TWO: (*As* JUDGE) Objection sustained.

ONE: The mistaken removal of the said tooth . . .

TWO: Was made by Mr. Fang,

ONE: On account of his vision having been previously impaired by the said Squint.

TWO: Justice, m'lud, justice!

ONE: (*As* JUDGE) Let justice be done.

TWO: Mr. Fang. (FANG *steps forward and impairs* SQUINT'S *vision*)

ONE: Thus you have heard it said . . .

TWO: An eye for an eye, . . .

ONE: A tooth for a tooth, . . .

TWO: A nose for a nose, . . .

ONE: And so on . . .

TWO: And so forth.

ONE: But . . .

TWO: No buts. There are no exceptions.

ONE: But . . .

TWO: Aa! aa!

ONE: What about what Jesus says?

TWO: What *does* He say?

ONE: He says, 'Do not take revenge.'

TWO: Are you sure?

ONE: Yes. Look at this. (*Producing paper from notes*)

TWO: Let me see. (*Crosses stage*) Good Heavens! He's right. He does. He says . . . (*Returns to his position*)

ONE: If anyone strikes you on the right cheek . . . (FANG *and* SQUINT, *without their props, step forward as characters* A *and* B. A *strikes* B *on right cheek*)

TWO: Turn to him the other one also. (A *strikes* B *on left cheek. Pause.* B *kicks* A *hard on shin*)

ONE: Erm, I'm sorry.

TWO: (*To* B.) To turn the other cheek . . .

ONE: And then to kick your adversary on the shin . . .

TWO: Is fulfilling the letter of the passage . . .

ONE: Rather than the spirit. (B *looks disconsolate*)

TWO: Do not resist one who is evil.

ONE: Quite categorically, *not*.

TWO: To continue.

ONE: You have heard it said . . .

TWO: Love your neighbour. (A *and* B *exchange friendly glances over garden fence*)

ONE: And hate your enemy. (*they threaten each other with machine guns*)

TWO: But I say to you . . .

ONE: Love your enemy. (B *puts down gun*)

TWO: Do good to them that hate you. (B *pulls out handkerchief and begins polishing* A's *gun*)

ONE: Pray for those who persecute you. (B *kneels*)

TWO: 'Father, forgive them, for they don't know what they're doing.'

ONE: If you are to be seen (A *and* B *sit down again*)

TWO: As the sons of your Father in Heaven . . .

ONE: You must show the family likeness.

TWO: For He makes the sun rise . . .

ONE: On the evil . . . (B *gets up looking evil*)

TWO: And on the good. (A *jumps up with beatific smile*)

ONE: He sends rain on the just . . . (A *has prudently brought an umbrella. He opens it*)

TWO: And the unjust. (B *steals the umbrella*)

ONE: Man thinks only in terms of justice. (*The* JUDGE *steps forward and restores umbrella to* A)

TWO : But if you only love those who love you
      (*Indicating* A *and the* JUDGE)

ONE : What's so good about that?

TWO : God thinks supremely in terms of love.
      (*They invite* B *to join them under the
      umbrella*)
      (*During this final section the three figures in
      the mime become a chorus of different
      voices, raising objections to the standard of
      love. The* JUDGE *has become voice* C. *They
      speak to the audience*)

  A : But I find we're so different in
      temperament.

ONE : Love him.

  C : You see, we just don't get on.

TWO : Love him.

  B : She and I have a completely different way
      of going about things.

ONE : Love her.

  C : I find young people are so selfish.

TWO : Love them.

  B : I'll never forgive her for leaving me.

ONE : Forgive her, love her.

  A : I find it very hard to believe those people
      are Christians.

TWO : Love them.

  B : They know all about the Bible, those
      people, but what they don't know . . .

ONE : Love them.

  B : But . . .

TWO : No buts. There are no exceptions.

  B : But . . .

ONE : Aa! aa!

TWO : Be perfect.

ONE : As your Heavenly Father . . .

TWO : Is perfect.

Spreading the Word Around a Bit

GEOFF; ANDREW; MICHAEL, *members of the same church fellowship*

The Bible has some stern things to say about the subject of gossip. In the letter to the church at Rome, Paul numbers gossips among those who 'did not see fit to acknowledge God'; they 'reveal secrets' and 'say what they should not'. Gossip might well be seen as one of the 'little foxes' that destroy the vineyard of the church. It is therefore a satiric target that is well worth hitting hard, particularly by avoiding the stereotyped attitude that this is a female problem – men are equally guilty. Many of the things said in this sketch might seem innocuous enough, but the destructive power of gossip is so often covered by a well-meaning veneer, achieving its end by hints, half-truths and subtleties of motive and expression.

GEOFF, ANDREW *and* MICHAEL *enter and stand facing away from the audience towards the back of the stage. They remain in these positions except when they come forward to speak.* GEOFF *and* ANDREW *turn to the audience. They are in mid conversation.*

GEOFF: Look, you won't say anything, Andrew, will you? Because Gill would be really upset.

ANDREW: Of course.

GEOFF: If people knew . . .

ANDREW: Well, they mustn't.

GEOFF: I just wanted you to know, that's all.

ANDREW: Right.

GEOFF: I wish I knew what to do.

ANDREW: It's extremely hard to know. There seem to be so many problems around these days. Michael had a very serious disagreement with Brian the other day. They were at each others throats.

GEOFF: Michael!

ANDREW: Oh yes.

GEOFF: Good grief, I'd never have guessed it of him.

ANDREW: I'd never have guessed it of him either – I was told. Still, I think he's sorted it all out now. Just.

GEOFF: How do you mean 'just'?

ANDREW: Well, Michael's so . . .

GEOFF: Yes, I know what you mean.

ANDREW: I wouldn't want to give you the wrong impression, Geoff. Michael's a really nice guy, but you just don't know where you are with him.

GEOFF: It's strange you should say that, because I've been a little uneasy about Michael sometimes. I remember him at that house-party.

ANDREW: That's a very good example of what I'm talking about. (*Their conversation fades off.* MICHAEL *steps forward to join* ANDREW)

MICHAEL: I hear Geoff won't be with us on Tuesday, Andrew.

ANDREW: No, I don't think he will, Michael.

MICHAEL: Is he all right?

ANDREW: I think it's fair to say he's been under attack recently.

MICHAEL: I gather it's been a difficult year.

ANDREW: On and off. He shared quite a lot with me last night, actually.

MICHAEL: Did he?

ANDREW: Yes. It's a difficult thing to face on one's own. I don't know, but I think he was encouraged by what I said.

MICHAEL: It's been pretty grim, so Doreen tells me.

ANDREW: Oh, you know a bit about the situation, then?

MICHAEL: Only what I've gleaned here and there. The odd comment.

ANDREW: In that case you've probably gathered–

MICHAEL: Sonia?

ANDREW: Well, she's involved. A lot of it does surround her. Look, Michael, this is obviously only for your ears and prayers, but the other night things blew up again.

MICHAEL: Really? (*They turn away, still talking, as* GEOFF *steps forward to join* MICHAEL)

GEOFF: It's incredible!

MICHAEL: I don't know how he justifies it.

GEOFF: A hundred quid!

MICHAEL: Easily.

GEOFF: Just for the skis.

MICHAEL: On top of hotels, food, ski passes, rail fares . . .

GEOFF: No, they both flew. And the children.

MICHAEL: Right, well, we're obviously talking about five or six hundred quid.

GEOFF: Each.

MICHAEL: Where on earth does Andrew get all his money from?

GEOFF: I dunno. They're always talking about not having enough.

MICHAEL: No wonder, is it?

GEOFF: I think it's thoroughly irresponsible.

MICHAEL: (*Pause*) Why did they ask him to be a lay preacher?

GEOFF: Wouldn't have been my choice.

MICHAEL: Still, he's got his good side.

GEOFF: But he's hardly ever at home with his family, you know. (*At this point,* ANDREW *steps forward on the other side of* MICHAEL, *who freezes. As each pair speak, they*

*punctuate the ends of their remarks by
miming the tearing off and eating of morsels
of flesh from the third. In each case the
'victim' stands motionless between his as-
sailants. While maintaining a conversa-
tional tone, the accompanying actions should
be savage)*

GEOFF: You just don't know where you are with
someone like Michael.

ANDREW: I wouldn't want to give you the wrong
impression.

MICHAEL: I gather it's been a difficult year for Geoff.

ANDREW: He's been really under attack recently.

MICHAEL: He wouldn't have been my choice.

GEOFF: I think he's thoroughly irresponsible.

GEOFF: I'm a bit concerned about Michael's
attitude.

ANDREW: He's just out to please himself.

MICHAEL: Geoff's faith used to be so strong.

ANDREW: Things seem to be going from bad to
worse.

MICHAEL: Andrew was the one I always turned to
for advice.

GEOFF: Funny the way things have changed.

How to be a Hero (Gideon: The Early Years)

NARRATOR; GIDEON, *a young man somewhat lacking in physical presence*; ANGEL

This sketch is an interlude from The Grand Slam, *commissioned by the* Pathfinders, *and to be published in due course. The story of Gideon stands on its own as a sketch and has been performed by* Riding Lights *as part of its repertoire. Although written for children, it works equally well for an adult audience.*

Enter NARRATOR.

NARRATOR: Good evening. Here is the good news. No one is ever too small or too weak or too insignificant to work for the King of Kings. Take the story of Gideon for a start – Gideon was the youngest member of the smallest family in the least important tribe of Israel. (*Enter* GIDEON, *nervously*)

GIDEON: Hello, I'm . . . er . . . well, (*Clearing his throat*) Gideon, actually. (*He laughs nervously*)

NARRATOR: But God chose Gideon to defeat the terrifying enemy, the Midianites!

GIDEON: (*Wheeling round*) Who me? (*The* ANGEL *enters*)

ANGEL: Yes, you.

GIDEON: (*Jumping back*) But . . . but . . . but . . . but have you seen the Midianites! Well, I suppose, being an angel you have seen the Midianites, ha, ha! But the point is, and this is where the crunch comes, those

fellows are *big*, and when I say big, I
mean – telephone directories in half, you
know the stuff, and I . . . Well, quite
honestly, I'm not even a seven stone
weakling, I'm only six and a half stone
weakling and today is Tuesday.

ANGEL: Tuesday?

GIDEON: (*Sitting down*) Yes. Tuesday is my day off.

ANGEL: Gideon. Get up at once.

GIDEON: Yessir.

ANGEL: Now stop wasting time. When I say I
want *you* to blast the Midianites into
smithereens, I mean *you*! Right?

GIDEON: Right!

ANGEL: You!

GIDEON: Me! . . . Right! Fine! . . . (*Beginning to go
and then turning back*) Just one question.

ANGEL: What?

GIDEON: What about if I have measles?

ANGEL: Gideon, you do not have measles.

GIDEON: No. But I really wish I did have measles.

ANGEL: Gideon, even if you did have measles,
you would still have to go and FIGHT
THE MIDIANITES!

GIDEON: (*Going*) Right! Fight the . . . Midianites.
Right! (*Turning*) One more question.

ANGEL: (*Wearily*) What is it?

GIDEON: How do I know that all this isn't a joke,
a sort of sick joke, you know, let's have a
bit of a laugh, let's send that weedy,
skinny little Gideon to fight the Midianites and watch him get hacked to pieces
and all have a jolly good laugh. I mean, I
wouldn't blame you. I'd be the first to
make a total and utter fool out of
somebody like me – now don't get me
wrong – I just want a little bit of proof,
that's all I'm asking, so . . . say I, er . . .

lay out this sheepskin on the grass (*He takes off his sheepskin jacket*) and in the morning, there's dew on the sheepskin but not on the grass. That would be a miracle, right?

ANGEL: Right!

GIDEON: That would be proof, right?

ANGEL: Right!

GIDEON: Okay.

NARRATOR: So Gideon laid out the sheepskin and went to bed. (GIDEON *mimes winding up his alarm clock, cleaning his teeth and going to sleep*) And in the morning: Brrrrring! (GIDEON *wakes up, stops the alarm and checks the fleece*)

GIDEON: Curses! A miracle! Which means, you're right, I've got to fight the Midianites. Okay. Fair enough. But to fight the Midianites, people like me have got to be very sure that the Lord is on their side. So, what do you say, we try it the other way round – dew on the grass and not on the fleece? And it's a deal.

ANGEL. Done.

NARRATOR: So Gideon went back to bed. (GIDEON *mimes winding up the alarm, cleaning his teeth, then says his prayers – pointing to the sheepskin and shaking his head – clearly praying that there won't be a miracle this time. He goes to sleep*) And sure enough, in the morning: Brrrring! (GIDEON *wakes up, stops the alarm, and checks the sheepskin. Then he checks the ground. He double checks. Then he crosses over his hands and tries checking the sheepskin and the ground with a different hand.*)

GIDEON: Curses! Another miracle!

NARRATOR: So Gideon had to go and fight the

Midianites.

GIDEON: Right. I'm getting a bodyguard. A body-guard of fifty thousand men. (GIDEON *stands at the side of the stage and shouts orders to an imaginary vast army offstage. He makes the sound of their tramping and improvises other army effects*)

ANGEL: Er . . . Gideon?

GIDEON: Squaaaaaaad halt! (*He makes the sound of soldiers standing to attention*) Yup?

ANGEL: Where are you going?

GIDEON: Just going to fight the Midianites.

ANGEL: Who are they?

GIDEON: Who?

ANGEL: Those soldiers.

GIDEON: (*Looking round, seeing his army as if by surprise and jumping back*) Ohhh! Oh *those* soldiers . . . er . . . er . . . some friends, you know . . . going to help, a few old school chums, ha, ha!

ANGEL: Gideon, no school has that many pupils.

GIDEON: Comprehensive educa. . .?
(*His voice trails off into a nervous cough*)

ANGEL: Gideon, the Lord finds that huge army an insult to his power. Get rid of it.

GIDEON: Er, right. (*He looks at his imaginary army offstage and mimes dismissing three or four soldiers*)

ANGEL: Just keep a few.

GIDEON: What?

ANGEL: A *few*.

GIDEON: Er, right. (*He mimes recalling the three or four soldiers and dismissing the huge army.* GIDEON *and the* ANGEL *leave*)

NARRATOR: Well, it's a very long story but the Lord proved his point. Gideon, the youngest member of the smallest family in the least important tribe of Israel, with a handful

of men, utterly defeated the Midianites.
POW!! (GIDEON *leaps back onstage and
throws his cap in the air*)

GIDEON: I don't know my own strength – (*He
pounds his chest and hurts himself*) or,
rather – the Lord's strength, ha, ha!

NARRATOR: And rescued Israel. LONG LIVE
GIDEON!

GIDEON: It was nothing actually, well – when I say
nothing, I do of course mean, it was really
quite something that God should use *me*,
you know, ha, ha!

NARRATOR: So that is the good news: the weaker you
are, the smaller you are, the more insignificant you feel, the more the God of all
creation wants to take your life and make
it dynamite!!

The Examination

FOUR DEVILS: DR. CUNNINGHAM, *young female*; PROFESSOR
TWIST, *suave, middle-aged*; DR. GLOAT, *pinched, middle-aged
woman*; DR. leFACTS, *eccentric and octogenarian*; J. S. NICHOLL,
a hesitant Christian

*Temptation is not an easy subject to deal with in a way that is
educational as well as entertaining. In* The Screwtape Letters,
*C. S. Lewis has memorably and perceptively satirised the works
of the Devil, with many flashes of wit and humour, albeit of a
somewhat chilling nature. At the beginning of the book, he
quotes Martin Luther: 'The best way to drive out the devil, if
he will not yield to texts of Scripture, is to jeer and flout him, for
he cannot bear scorn.' In a similar way, this sketch uses humour
to illuminate a very serious subject, for temptation leads to sin,
which leads to death, and it is this Biblical equation on which
the sketch finally turns. Jesus refuted the temptations in the
wilderness by quoting the written Word of God, and thorough
knowledge of the Bible is still a primary weapon against the
devil today.*

*The scene will be particularly familiar to students since it is set
in a university 'viva voce', or oral examination. Four chairs are
placed on three sides of a large table, on which there is a
telephone. Another chair is set facing the table at an angle, but
isolated from it. Enter* PROFESSOR TWIST, DR. GLOAT *and* DR.
leFACTS *in academic dress, carrying sheaves of paper. They sit
around the table, impatiently waiting for* DR. CUNNINGHAM *to
fill the fourth chair. After a pause, she enters.*

CUNNINGHAM: No apologies for being late, Professor.
(*Sits*)

TWIST: Bad, bad. Well, I suppose we'd better get
a move on. The world may be drawing to
a close and we've got all these people to

tempt before the Last Judgement. Now, who've we got next?

GLOAT: Excuse me, Professor, but I do find Earth rather chilly. Can we do anything about it?

TWIST: Try a bit of hell*fire*, I suppose. (*General chuckles*) Perhaps Dr. leFacts would care to lend you his gown, though I realise it's hardly within his nature to do so?

leFACTS: (*Chuckling*) Not likely.

TWIST: Bad. Shall we proceed? Our next candidate appears to be J. S. Nicholl. I trust you have his papers in front of you.

CUNNINGHAM: Shall I call him in, Professor?

TWIST: Why not? He should be suitably nervous by now.

GLOAT: Before you do, Inferna, am I not right in thinking that this person is a Christian? (*General groans*) So it, er, might be a little trickier than the last one.

TWIST: Hell's bells. (*Phone rings*) Hullo? (*Covering phone*) Talk of the devil. (*Back to phone*) Yes, sir, of course, sir. We were just about to begin the temptation when you rang. Oh, really? That's very bad of you. Aha, mmm. Well, thank you for being so impatient with us. (*Makes face at phone as he hangs up. It burns his hand*)

CUNNINGHAM: I see the hot-line's still functional. Shall I get him now?

TWIST: Please. (CUNNINGHAM *exits and returns with* NICHOLL)
Ah, Nicholl.

NICHOLL: (*Correcting him*) J. Nicholl actually, sir. (*'We've got a right one here' looks from examiners*)

TWIST: Just sit down, Mr. Nicholl. Now, we've read your papers on Biblical Knowledge

with considerable disinterest and we
would like to ask you a few questions
arising out of your answers, if you see
what I mean? Fire away, then, chaps.

leFACTS: Do the words *Viva Voce* mean anything
to you, Mr. Nicholl?

NICHOLL: No, I'm afraid not.

leFACTS: No, I've never understood them myself.
Thank you, Professor.

GLOAT: Mr. Nicholl, what precise evidence do
you find in the Bible to support your
statement here that, I quote, 'God loves
you'?

NICHOLL: Well, er, yes, there's a famous verse, erm
. . . somewhere in Matthew, I think . . .

GLOAT: 'Somewhere in Matthew'. How deli-
ciously vague. Can you quote it, Mr.
Nicholl?

NICHOLL: No. I'm sorry.

GLOAT: Oh, please. Don't start being *sorry* for
anything here. (*Much chuckling among
examiners*)

leFACTS: (*Highly amused*) 'Sorry', ahaha!

TWIST: (*Trying to recover a sense of seriousness*)
Mr. Nicholl, can you explain why your
answer on the miracles of Jesus made no
reference to the miracle of the bricks
being turned into water?

NICHOLL: I don't recall ever reading that one, sir.

TWIST: Come, come, Mr. Nicholl, surely you
have read the Gospel according to
Norman?

NICHOLL: I don't think so, sir.

TWIST: It comes just after Luke.

CUNNINGHAM: You'll find it a lot less helpful than some
of the others.

TWIST: Did you have a question, Dr.
Cunningham?

CUNNINGHAM: Yes. (*Posing provocatively on edge of table. Speaking huskily*) Mr. Nicholl, how do you understand the concept of temptation?

GLOAT: I doubt that he will fall for anything as obvious as that, Inferna.

CUNNINGHAM: There's no point in making things too subtle, sweetie, this one's hardly been known to fail. (*Resuming husky voice*) Mr. Nicholl?

NICHOLL: (*Sweating*) Well, erm, temptation is an external pressure on the individual conscience, which – well, internal, too, I suppose – a pressure to deviate . . .

CUNNINGHAM: Yes?

NICHOLL: To deviate from what one believes to be fundamentally true; truth being something which is defined and received from God and contained in His Word.

CUNNINGHAM: And who told you all that, Mr. Nicholl?

NICHOLL: God did.

CUNNINGHAM: God *speaks* to you? Fascinating. How?

NICHOLL: Through His Word.

CUNNINGHAM: But who told you *that*, Mr. Nicholl?

NICHOLL: God did.

CUNNINGHAM: I see. Thank you, Professor.

leFACTS: (*Clearing throat*) Aren't we getting our wires crossed a little here, Mr. Nicholl? I must say I'm very surprised to hear you speak of the Bible as, shall we say, the Fountain-head of Truth. Perhaps in your studies, wide though your reading may have been, you have overlooked my colleague Professor Twist's own work on Biblical inconsistency. Do you not find any evidence for this in, say, the Book of Proverbs?

NICHOLL: I can't say that I've ever considered it.

leFACTS: Well, er, 'Too many cooks spoil the broth', yet, 'Many hands make light work'. I mean, what do you make of it?

NICHOLL: Are those both *in* Proverbs, sir?

leFACTS: You tell me, Mr. Nicholl, after all, it is not I who am being examined, is it?

NICHOLL: I'm afraid I don't know the answer, sir.

TWIST: You must avoid being too honest in your replies, Mr. Nicholl. Now, I should like to move on to another question. Would you say that material prosperity has ever influenced your academic career?

NICHOLL: (*Sharply*) No.

TWIST: It's all right, it's all right. Just tempting.

GLOAT: Your overall haziness of the Book of Proverbs prompts me to ask another question. Your written answers make almost exclusive reference to material drawn from the New Testament, in particular the Epistles. Do you only read the short ones, Mr. Nicholl?

NICHOLL: I have read the Old Testament.

GLOAT: Summarise for me the message of the book of Deuteronomy.

NICHOLL: That's near the beginning, isn't it? Well, it's . . . um . . .

GLOAT: You're doing very well Mr. Nicholl.

NICHOLL: It's about Moses and the Israelites and sacrificing.

TWIST: Have you ever thought of publishing your research, Mr. Nicholl. I mean, I think you can afford to take considerable pride in your work. At least, you'll certainly be able to afford it once you've published. (*Shares private joke*) Ahem. Fine. Why didn't you answer the question on the irrelevance of prayer?

NICHOLL: I had already answered three questions

and I happen to find it very relevant.

TWIST: The question?

NICHOLL: No, prayer.

TWIST: But you haven't answered my question, Mr. Nicholl.

NICHOLL: I have answered your question.

TWIST: Am I making you angry?

NICHOLL: Yes.

TWIST: Good.

CUNNINGHAM: Mr. Nicholl, would you mind completing the quotation, 'the wages of sin are . . .'?

NICHOLL: Um . . . er . . .

CUNNINGHAM: Bad?

leFACTS: Low, compared with the national average? (*General chuckling*)

NICHOLL: That's not right. It's 'the wages of sin *is* . . .', you've misquoted it.

CUNNINGHAM: That's what we're here for.

NICHOLL: 'The wages of sin is death.' (*All four examiners sit up sharply, drawing in breath and glaring at* NICHOLL. *There is an icy atmosphere*)

leFACTS: No need to overstate it, Mr. Nicholl.

TWIST: That sort of knowledge won't get you very far, will it?

GLOAT: That will probably be all for now, Professor.

CUNNINGHAM: What a pity we had to end on such an awkward note.

TWIST: Thank you, Mr. Nicholl. Don't hesitate to be in touch if we can be of any further hindrance to you. The results will be published in due course. (*Exit* NICHOLL. *Lights fade out on the* DEVILS *bickering and muttering together over the table*)

In the Nick of Time

NARRATOR ONE; NARRATOR TWO; *characters in the mime*: A
GROUSE; A GROUSE-SHOOTER; TWO CHRISTIANS; TWO ROMAN
SOLDIERS; PETER, *the apostle*; FIGURE IN NIGHTMARE; ANGEL;
SEVERAL MEMBERS OF PRAYER-GROUP, (*optional*); SERVANT-
GIRL

Read the instructions to 'AN EYE FOR AN EYE' (*page 93*). *If the
cast list of this sketch looks daunting, the characters in the
mime could be played by three or four actors, using 'different
hats' and making swift changes behind a central screen. Most
of the movements of the mime must be left to the imagination
and ingenuity of the director. The* 'PRAYER-GROUP *is optional
in that it can be suggested convincingly by the* NARRATORS'
*dialogue. The sketch has also been performed very successfully
with the various characters speaking their lines, where
appropriate.*

> ONE: The most exciting . . .
> TWO: Dynamic . . .
> ONE: Radical . . .
> TWO: Far-reaching . . .
> ONE: And fundamental . . .
> TWO: Changes in the history of the Church . . .
> ONE: Have stemmed . . .
> TWO: Almost entirely . . .
> ONE: From grouse-hunting.
> TWO: What's that?
> ONE: Grouse-hunting.
> TWO: What do you mean?
> ONE: (*Insistently trying to reassure*) It's all right,
>   everything's under control.
> TWO: But, but . . .
> ONE: This is a grouse. (*Enter* GROUSE)
> TWO: (*Groans*)

ONE: 'I'm thoroughly fed up!'

TWO: BANG! (*Enter* GROUSE-SHOOTER)

ONE: 'One to me, Maurice.' (GROUSE *is dragged off*)

TWO: (*Coughs*) Has this anything to do with the Early Church?

ONE: Apparently.

TWO: Well, I have here, 'The Importance of House-meetings in The Early Church.'

ONE: Oh, *house*-meetings, not *grouse*-meetings?

TWO: No.

ONE: Ah, I see. I'm with you.

TWO: You've done it now.

ONE: No, wait, there's a perfect link. Listen.

TWO: Go on.

ONE: (*Beginning again*) Of all the sports in the Roman Empire . . .

TWO: The most popular was . . .

ONE: Hunt-the-Christian. (*Enter* CHRISTIAN)

TWO: (*Singing*) 'And can it be that I should –'

ONE: DUMPF! (CHRISTIAN *is knocked senseless by a* ROMAN SOLDIER *who has crept up behind him*)

TWO: 'One to me, Suetonius.' (*Body is dragged off*)

ONE: Life in the Early Church was never dull. (*Enter* SECOND CHRISTIAN)

TWO: It was challenging . . .

ONE: Inspiring . . .

TWO: Frequently brief . . .

ONE: And to the point. (CHRISTIAN *is summarily despatched with smart sword-thrust from* SECOND ROMAN SOLDIER)

TWO: 'One all, Marcellus.'

ONE: To be a Roman soldier in those days . . .

TWO: Was a demanding business.

ONE: It required skill . . .

TWO: Courage . . .

ONE: And great presence of mind. (*Exit* SOLDIER)

TWO: To be an apostle in those days . . . (*Enter* PETER)

ONE: Required faith . . .

TWO: Hope . . .

ONE: And considerable trust in God.

TWO: Such a man was Peter.

ONE: He confronted the Pharisees . . .

TWO: He confounded the lawyers . . .

ONE: He confused the authorities . . .

TWO: He converted the heathen . . .

ONE: And was clapped into jail. (NARRATORS *applaud*)

TWO: But throughout all this, as Head of the Church . . .

ONE: Peter was bald and hairless. (*Rechecking script*) I'm sorry, bold and fearless.

TWO: The Romans had bagged a big one.

ONE: Guarded by four squads of soldiers . . .

TWO: Handcuffed to his jailers . . .

ONE: Locked . . .

TWO: And double-locked, . . .

ONE: Peter lay in the deepest dungeon . . .

ONE: Under sentence of death.

ONE: Now over to our sportsdesk in Rome.

TWO: Gladiators – 37.

ONE: Other gladiators – nil.

TWO: Lions – $52\frac{1}{2}$.

ONE: Christians – $\frac{1}{2}$.

TWO: For Peter . . .

ONE: Things looked bleak.

TWO: Nonetheless, at the box-office, they looked good.

ONE: Peter's friends were justifiably alarmed.

TWO: That night they gathered for prayer.

ONE: They prayed fervently . . .

TWO: Earnestly . . .

ONE: With tears . . .

TWO: And sighs.

ONE: Imploring . . .

TWO: Beseeching . . .

ONE: Pleading . . .

TWO: Covering the situation with a mighty shield of intercession.

ONE: Pardon?

TWO: Sorry. So they prayed . . .

ONE: And prayed . . .

TWO: And prayed.

ONE: They just prayed, Lord, that God would surround Peter with His love, Father.

TWO: So He did.

ONE: They just prayed that if it be Thy Will, Lord, . . .

TWO: Thou wouldst in some special way, . . .

ONE: Perhaps, . . .

TWO: Bless this situation, Father.

ONE: So He did.

TWO: They just prayed that in a very real sense,

ONE: O Lord, . . .

TWO: Though humanly speaking it was hard to see how, . . .

ONE: God would encourage Peter through His angels and ministers of light.

TWO: So He did. (*Figure enters prison where* PETER *is lying beside his jailer*)

ONE: 'Pssst!'

TWO: (*As* PETER) 'Whassat!?'

ONE: 'It's me going "pssst".'

TWO: 'Who are you?'

ONE: 'The Pssst-man. Bye.' (*Exit* FIGURE)

TWO: Peter had many similar nightmares.

ONE: So when God sent an angel. (*Enter* ANGEL)

TWO: He thought he was dreaming.

ONE: But his chains fell off and woke him up.

TWO: 'Good Heavens!' said Peter.

ONE: 'Precisely,' said the angel.

TWO: 'But how?' said Peter.

ONE: 'Airmail,' said the angel.

TWO: 'Sorry to be so bright and early.'

ONE: 'Hang on, I'll turn myself off.'

TWO: (*Click*) (ANGEL *reduces glare from halo*)

ONE: 'Thanks.'

TWO: 'Now follow me,' said the angel.

ONE: 'It is *Peter*, isn't it?'

TWO: 'Yes.'

ONE: 'Cell forty-one?'

TWO: 'Yes'.

ONE: 'Right, follow me.'

TWO: Past the guards . . .

ONE: Through the doors . . .

TWO: Down the steps . . .

ONE: Across the courtyard . . .

TWO: Through the iron gates . . .

ONE: And into the streets of the city.

TWO: 'Sign here,' said the angel.

ONE: 'What for?'

TWO: 'Recorded delivery.'

ONE: 'Stand by for take-off.'

TWO: 'Right-o, Algie.'

ONE: 'Over and out.'

TWO: (*Noise of sudden airborne departure*) (*Exit* ANGEL)

ONE: Peter came to himself.

TWO: 'Hullo. Is that Peter?'

ONE: 'Yes.'

TWO: 'Follow me.'

ONE: (*To other narrator*) Shut up.

TWO: Sorry.

ONE: Soon he arrived outside the house where his friends were praying.

TWO: He knocked loudly.

ONE: (*Knocking*)

TWO: O Lord, we do just continue to pray,

Father, . . .

ONE: That you will come to our brother Peter in his cell . . .

TWO: Encouraging him . . .

ONE: Supporting him . . .

TWO: Assuring him that he has not been forgotten.

ONE: (*Knocking*)

TWO: And let us not be distracted, Lord.

ONE: (*Knocking*)

TWO: Lord, as You look down on Peter now, . . .

ONE: We pray, Father, that You will hear his cry.

TWO: 'Open up!'

ONE: And Lord, whoever that is, . . .

TWO: Calm him . . .

ONE: And give him your peace.

TWO: 'LET ME IN!'

ONE: And so, as Peter stood knocking at the door, . . .

TWO: A servant-girl had the sense to answer it.

ONE: 'Who is it?'

TWO: (*As if through letterbox*) 'Peter.'

ONE: She recognised his voice.

TWO: Her heart leapt into her mouth.

ONE: (*Gulp*)

TWO: Her legs turned to jelly.

ONE: (*Fllobbalobalob*)

TWO: She ran back to the prayer-meeting.

ONE: 'It's Peter! It's Peter!'

TWO: O Lord, we do ask – what's that?

ONE: 'It's Peter!'

TWO: Yes, dear, we're praying for him.

ONE: 'Shall I let him in?'

TWO: Not now, dear, we're praying for Peter.

ONE: 'He's standing outside.'

TWO: Ask him for two pints and we'll pay him on Thursday.

ONE: (*Knocking*)

TWO: 'OPEN UP!!'

ONE: 'I told you, it's Peter!'

TWO: You're mad.

ONE: (*Knocking*)

TWO: 'IT'S ME, PETER!'

ONE: You know what?

TWO: What?

ONE: That sounds like Peter outside.

TWO: The very thing we were praying for. Hallelujah.

ONE: Hallelujah.

TWO: Praise the Lord!

ONE: 'WILL YOU LET ME IN!'

TWO: Oh, yes. So they did.

ONE: Now when you turn to prayer,

TWO: Remember that He's there.

ONE: His angels know the score,

TWO: They've been down here before.

PLANNING PRODUCTIONS AND WORKSHOPS

The effectiveness of any theatrical performance depends to a large extent on the precision, discipline and control which the director and the actors are able to bring to their work, both in rehearsal and in the performance itself. Similarly, before the first performance takes place, there are many issues that need careful thought and preparation, if that point is to be reached successfully, even in the case of performing a single sketch in a church service. Workshops, too, need an organised structure, planned by a capable leader, in order to be *work*shops rather than *talk*shops, or worse still, *dribble-about-and-then-we-went-home-but-it-was-quite-fun*shops. The intention of this section is to offer some simple suggestions which may be of assistance to those responsible for the organisation of a drama group or a production. Obviously, some of these suggestions refer to productions beyond the scope of the material in this book and others will seem self-evident to certain readers. The end result is a basic manual, where points can be ignored or taken note of as is appropriate.

Producing sketches

All of the sketches in this book, with the exception of 'The Next Sketch' (p. 58), could be performed on their own, though it is hard to think of many contexts where an isolated sketch would be very apt. Many of them would work much better used as illustrative material in something longer – a school assembly, a sermon, a talk or in place of a reading from the Bible in a church service. However, even the production of one sketch for this kind of use requires more than the learning of lines and the blocking of moves. As well as the cast, a director and a stagemanager should be appointed. The stagemanager for a sketch might well be someone within the cast, who will take full responsibility for all props and costumes being in the right place at the right time and for actors turning up and the performance taking place, also at the right time. Once the piece is rehearsed, the time and venue of the performance fixed, consideration must be given to *sightlines* for the audience (especially if seated, kneeling or recumbent actors will not be seen by more than the first few rows), to the question of *audibility* (in some venues a PA system may be necessary), to *cues* for the beginning and end of your piece (also check that whoever is *introducing* you knows what is going to happen and will therefore do this sensitively and, above all, briefly; if possible give your own introduction), to the *setting* and *striking* of props, to the nature of your *audience* (it is possible that an occasional change of a line or detail in the script might sharpen the relevance of the performance for a particular group or situation; e.g. the objections from the characters at the end of 'An Eye for an Eye' (p. 93) could be altered, to make them fit a local context. N.B. This should only be done if there is a specific advantage to be gained.). Hopefully, you will be able to give your audience confidence in your performance, by being confident yourselves. Where someone else is involved, perhaps giving a talk around or after the sketch, always make sure they have seen it in rehearsal – this saves the embarrassment of them not knowing quite what to say next or even dismissing it with, 'Well, that was very powerful/telling/amusing, wasn't it? Now back to my sermon.' If thorough attention is paid to every detail, the five-minute sketch can be 'a gem'.

Many groups, as they develop, will be given increasing opportunities to perform whole programmes of sketches. The choice of programme should be conditioned, first of all, by the nature of the audience and the style of the venue and then by the capabilities of your group (which are your strongest sketches, etc.?). The arranging of a programme requires experience and experiment and since you will ultimately be the best judges of your own work, the following outlines ought not to be regarded as successful blueprints but more as indications of the way a sequence of sketches can be tailored, paced and linked together in the most effective combination. Most of the sketches referred to are in this present selection, but for breadth and variety, we have included some sketches from our other book *Time to Act* (also published by Hodder and Stoughton): these are asterisked. 'Linking' by a compère or by members of the cast is obviously optional, but it can give coherence to the programme and even add to it, if this job is done in a relaxed manner, with the odd joke or humorous anecdote thrown in here and there. Needless to say, the best linking will always be brief and well rehearsed. The links below are again, like the sequences, only suggestions and many other, different points could be made from the sketches – it all depends on the overall theme and object of the performance.

A possible programme for street-theatre

Objective: To gather a crowd and to entertain them for about half an hour with something of the truth and vitality of the Gospel.

Method: Make a very lively start, full of noise, colour and action. (You might even precede the sketches with a vigorously 'performed' song-and-dance or some impromptu advertising.) Move on through one or two sketches of a general nature, which are fast and funny (definitely nothing 'heavy' at this stage). Bridge towards the heart of your message with a sketch which points to the person of Jesus. Deliver your message of Good News clearly and simply (the dramatic climax) and then maybe end off with something 'gentler', though still lively and humorous, to open the way for personal conversation with the audience afterwards.

Warnings: Always *obtain permission* for your performance. State clearly who you are and where you come from; people today are often suspicious of groups and sects 'button-holing' them on the streets. Don't try and perform for longer than half an hour, especially in winter; if anything, be shorter.

'Eternal Youth' (Link: Hello, and welcome. We are . . . from . . . A lot of people suffer from delusions these days, like the man who jumped off the Eiffel Tower with springs on his feet – he landed on his head. We may not always think we're young, but perhaps we always think we're wise. Here's a sketch about a wise man and a fool.)

'The House on the Rock'* (Link: That, believe it or not, is a story which Jesus told about what it means to be really wise – well, we changed the words a bit. But most of it's in the Bible. The Bible's a funny book, you know. It is. It's funny because it's *the* number one bestseller, and yet very few people read it. Excuse me . . . (*He is interrupted by the arrival of an army*).)

'General Conformity' (Link: Sorry about that interruption. Now where was I? Oh, yeah, the Bible. Now there was one guy who only just got into the Bible, but it was all right 'cos he was short, so they let him in. But that was only because someone spotted him up a tree, see? His name was Zacchaeus and one thing he wasn't short of – was cash.)

'Zacc's for Tax' (Link: You know the great thing about Jesus was that He had time for everyone. It didn't matter who they were or what they'd done. But it's no wonder that Zacchaeus felt a bit shy. I mean, we'd all be a bit shy if God came along and said, 'Hello.' But that's what happened, and this sketch explains why.)

'The Light of the World'* (Link: Jesus described Himself as the Light of the World, and if you feel that the world looks pretty dark and gloomy that could be because people aren't looking towards the Light. Zacchaeus got 'switched on' by the light of Jesus and so can we because Jesus is still alive and God is a God who can be trusted. That's the point of our final sketch – the story of David

and Goliath!)
'David and Goliath' (Don't hang around too long waiting
for applause. Get out and talk to them.)

A possible short programme on a theme

Objective: A coherent exploration through theatre of (in
these cases) Biblical teaching about one theme. Performance
to last about 20 to 25 minutes. Essentially for a Christian
audience.
Method: A relaxed, humorous beginning to allow the
audience to 'tune in' from whatever has just been happening
and to command their attention. Humour also helps to make
an audience feel less 'got at' by the teaching and therefore
readier to accept what God wants to say to them. Develop
the theme right from the start and ensure that all material
is relevant. Unlike street-theatre, you shouldn't have to be
too nervous of your audience drifting away (they may drift
off to sleep, but people seldom register their boredom in
church by walking out). However, you should still keep
varying the overall pace, following a long sketch with a
shorter one etc. In each of these two programmes, the most
'serious' piece comes third, though it is succeeded by a final
sketch which sustains and follows the climax through to a
conclusion.
N.B. The suggested linking here deliberately leaves more to
the imagination.

THEME 1 : DISCIPLESHIP
'How to be a Hero' (Link: God chooses his disciples
carefully. The weak to shame the strong. God's power is
seen more clearly. Anything which has a strong hold on
us has to go.)
'The Appointment'* (Link: Peter also discovered the cost
of discipleship)
'Question Time' (Link: Although he failed, Peter discovered
that the disciple is never alone, however alone he *feels*.

The Resurrection happened. Peter's courage was restored. But that first Easter, Mary Magdalene was coping with a different kind of loneliness.)
'Early One Morning'

THEME 2: THE TONGUE
'Snakes and Ladders'*
'Violence in the Home'*
'Spreading the Word Around a Bit' (Link: We've seen three different pictures of the damage that can be caused by our tongues. Whatever spills out of our mouths is whatever is in our hearts. Our hearts should be full of one thing, love.)
'An Eye for an Eye'

A possible programme for a full evening's entertainment

Objective: A full-scale performance, lasting around two hours (including an interval), to which friends/their guests/members of the public could be invited. (The audience is therefore somewhat mixed, but all are aware that they are coming to a performance organised by Christians; so don't start apologising for it, make your show as good as other attractions in your town.)

Method: After a good 'punchy' start, take people up to the interval with a series of sketches which will be entertaining, provide plenty of laughs and at the same time prepare the ground spiritually by commenting more on the condition of man and our attitudes, than on the person of Jesus or the character of God; this can come in the second half. A strong, 'up beat' ending before the interval, coming in again after it with a sketch to help people settle down. Build through the main theme and end the whole evening with a warm, friendly finish. The minimum of linking is probably best. The second half should be shorter than the first.

First Half
'Eternal Youth'
'Snakes and Ladders'*
'The Parable of the Talents'*
'General Conformity'
'The Next Sketch'
'Party Games'
'Here Beginneth the Second
   Lesson'
(*interval*)

Second Half
'The Parable of the Good
   Punk Rocker'*
'Importunity Knocks'*
'For the Good of the Team'
'The Light of the World'*
'Early One Morning'
'Angel Space'

The order of your sketches will also have to take into account any problematic costume changes for any member of the cast, and it must be stressed again that the orders illustrated above are there to demonstrate the *principles* behind constructing a show, not to provide one or two schemes to be endlessly rehashed. Not all the sketches have been included to leave room for experiment. A brief acquaintance with the material will show, for instance, that certain groups of sketches are especially relevant to some of the main festivals in the Church's calendar – Christmas, Palm Sunday, Easter etc.

Since some of the pieces in this book are deliberately looking beyond the limits of a simple sketch (in particular, 'A Funny Thing'), some guidance might be helpful for those who wish to negotiate the web of organisation that lies behind any successful large-scale production. The following should act as a basic checklist, though some of the points may not always apply.

A guide to planning a full-scale production

1. Choose the play. (Obvious, but fundamental)
2. Obtain permission to perform from the holders of the performing rights and ascertain the cost involved.
3. Check whether rights governing music, if any, are additional or included.

4. Decide on the venue and discover hire cost for the days of performance and prior time needed for 'fit-up' and final rehearsals.

5. Appoint the production team: director, administrator, production manager, stage manager, designer, wardrobe, lighting-board operator, sound operator, musical director and choreographer (if necessary).

6. Plan production budget. Work out your *estimated income* from:

   (i) Ticket sales at, say, 60% houses
  (ii) Sale of programmes
 (iii) Any donated income/project grants etc.
 (iv) Income from advertising sponsorship – e.g. local firms or restaurants using your publicity for advertisement.

Your BUDGET (*estimated expenditure*) can now be based on the total estimated income. Obviously, once you have costed the production, you may have to go back and readjust the ticket prices. Depending on the needs of the production, your budget may or may not include:

(a) *Staging* This could involve hire of scaffolding and purchase of flooring and a stagecloth.
(b) *Set*
    (i) Designer's fee
   (ii) Materials/paint etc.
  (iii) Fee for stage-carpenter(s)
(c) *Costumes and Props*
    (i) Designer's fee (if separate from above)
   (ii) Materials
  (iii) Hire of anything e.g. furniture, or particular period costumes
(d) *Lighting*
    (i) Designer's fee
   (ii) Hire of lanterns
  (iii) You may need help with rigging the lanterns. A local theatre technician will normally help for a consideration.

(iv) Secondary Lighting (This is essential for any building where an audience is paying to see a performance. You may need to provide your own. This is an emergency lighting system, run independently from the mains supply. This must be in operation from the time the audience enters, to the time the last person leaves.)

(e) *Special Effects* These can often be quite expensive, (e.g. ultra-violet light, strobe etc.)

(f) *Sound*
   (i) System for effects and music (in interval etc.)
   (ii) Microphones for singers/ off-stage voices
   (iii) Amplification for any band or accompaniment

(g) *Publicity*
   (i) Posters, handouts, programmes
   (ii) Design costs
   (iii) Classified adverts in local press
   (iv) Pre-publicity; press releases/photographs
   (v) Mailing possible clientele

(h) *Scripts* Copies of published works must be bought for actors, not duplicated or photocopied

(i) *Make-up*

(j) *Black-out material* Theatres shouldn't need this, churches invariably do

(k) *Ticket printing*

(l) *Refreshments*

(m) *Photographer* To come to the Dress Rehearsal or a special photo-call. Foyer prints etc. are useful publicity.

(n) *Administration costs* Stationery, telephone etc.

(o) *Cost of electricity and heating* This is normally included in the hire of the venue.

(p) *Contingency* Always allow a margin for last-minute things, which you will have forgotten – the director may suddenly want to do the whole production on ice, with live animals.

If this list looks daunting, don't forget that there are several things under 2, 3 and 4, which you may have already spent money on. Bad luck.

7. Plan Production Schedule. (The Production Manager organises the following and is responsible for the budget relating to:)

  (i) Deadline for set design
  (ii) Deadline for set construction/dressing/fit-up
 (iii) Deadline for costume design
 (iv) Deadlines for costumes and props (some may be needed early in rehearsals)
  (v) Date for erection of stage (if necessary)
 (vi) Fire-proofing of all drapes/curtains/canvas flats etc.
 (vii) Hire of lighting and sound
(viii) Rigging lighting, secondary lighting, and sound system
 (ix) Installing black-out facilities, exit signs etc.
  (x) Making sure that everything is fully operational for the Technical Run-through

8. Plan Rehearsal Schedule. (This should be done by the Director, with reference to the Production Manager and the Administrator.)

  (i) Auditions
  (ii) Rehearsals (Organised well in advance and duplicated out, so that actors need only come for their own scenes. Many professional productions rehearse six hours a day, five days a week, for three weeks. You will have to plan your overall period on the basis of availability and competence of your cast.)
 (iii) Costume parade (At least four days before first night)
 (iv) Plotting the lights
  (v) Full Technical Rehearsal ('Tech-run'. This is primarily to check sound and lighting cues, the setting and striking of props, and to uncover any technical problems, such as impossible costume changes, doors that won't open or blood capsules which refuse to burst and land quivering synthetically near the front row of the audience during the death scene.)
 (vi) Full Dress Rehearsal (This should work like a

performance, i.e. without interruption whatever disasters befall, as if an audience was present. You may need to schedule two dress-runs.)

(vii) Opening Night

9. Organise the following: (Work done by the Administrator. NB The Administrator's task is one of the most difficult – to be diligent, efficient and in control, whilst being perfectly happy for others to take the artistic limelight, requires a great gift.)

(i) Obtain theatre licence (This is necessary for any building where an audience is paying, and is obtained from local council offices. At least two clear exits from theatre to street are imperative.)

(ii) Contact Fire Prevention Officer at Fire Brigade (not 999!) and ask for his requirements over the production. He will give advice about seating arrangements, the number of audience allowed (this may affect the budget), secondary lighting etc. Arrange a visit from him, once all the scenery, lighting etc. have been installed. He will then give final permission for a paying audience to be admitted.

(iii) Arrange printing and distribution of all publicity. (See (g) under budget) Find sponsors for programme advertising. Print programme with acknowledgements to benefactors and those who have provided anything for the production. Print tickets.

(iv) Take overall charge of arranging rehearsal space and calls for the company, in cooperation with the Director.

(v) Appoint caterers for the refreshments.

(vi) Appoint Front of House Manager, stewards for each performance and arrange for the box-office to be manned, or tickets to be sold in advance at one or two local shops.

(vii) Keep a check on advance ticket sales and change publicity strategy, if necessary.

(viii) Arrange for complimentary tickets to be sent to local press/any other special people, such as the Director's aunt/girlfriend.

(ix) Arrange for photographer.

(x) Administrate the budget. This may well prove to be the hardest and most important task. Keep everyone strictly to their budget figures by regular checking, collecting receipts for expenditure and threatening them with blunt instruments. As far as finance goes, the Administrator rules. OK?

10. Make sure the play goes well, delights the critics, pleases its audience and contains some stunning performances (see 'David and Goliath' p. 88).

An introduction to workshops

A comprehensive treatment of ideas and approaches to workshops would be a whole book in itself and there are, in any case, several good ones in existence, which we don't propose to duplicate. However, some of the principles of workshops can be outlined and these, when developed in practice, will provide a theatrical framework on which the actor can base his craft.

Workshops should be the staple diet of any drama group which meets on a regular basis. Needless to say, even groups which only gather for the occasional performance will perform far more successfully, if they have spent time working together, improving their skills and experimenting – the main objectives of all workshops. A fundamental principle is that a workshop should have an overall structure and end with a sense of achievement. Even if an experiment fails, the group will still have the satisfaction of creative involvement, if each member has been aware of what they were working towards. This needs good planning and firm leadership. A planned series of workshops with a stable group will produce the best results.

The workshop is the actor's drawing-board, where the

qualities needed on stage can be thought out and acquired. The underlying purpose should be to help an actor feel at ease on stage, even in front of a critical audience. This sense of freedom and naturalness in performance is closely related to the confidence gained through working with colleagues in workshops. Therefore any idea of a competitive standard must be abolished. In the workshop, 'freedom' and absolute 'trust' are the key words. Each person should feel happy to 'have a go' at everything; no one should sit on the sidelines since the presence of an audience undermines the point of the session, and anyway, coping with psychological difficulties (such as self-consciousness), is all part of the process of training the actor. Some groups can also be disrupted by people who are obviously more talented than the rest and know it. They turn their gift into a problem for themselves and for the group by being unwilling to do the simple things and feeling that certain exercises are 'beneath them'. Such 'know-alls' should be gently, but firmly squashed, for everyone's sake. It is essential that an atmosphere be created, where, like Paul's vision of the Body of Christ, differing gifts and levels of talent can be mutually beneficial, each member offering what they are able, so that the end product is a group achievement and a group improvement. Nothing to do with food and drink, but the atmosphere should be akin to a party, where people are enjoying themselves, getting to know each other and prepared to play even the daftest games without inhibition; the main difference being that in the workshop, the party is highly organised and everything is done for a reason, which is explained – often after the exercise or improvisation has been completed.

It cannot be overstressed that constant work of a technical kind on control of the body and control of the voice is fundamental. Every workshop should begin with a sustained work-out/warm-up. (Many ideas and schemes for movement exercises, muscle relaxation and control, breathing exercises and vocal development can be found in the appropriate books, of which there are many. See the bibliography in

Time to Act p. 128 for several good examples.) Repeated work of this kind may be unpopular, but it is the only way to improve your primary skills.

There are many aspects of an actor's craft which can be dealt with in a workshop: ease of movement/gesture/posture on stage; involvement with a character; precise communication of feeling; relationship to other actors; working from the inside to the outside in playing and creating a role; the studying of accents/mimicry; communicating without words; immediate improvisation of a given situation; facial expression. These are all areas which are important and can be developed by games, exercises and improvisations. Again, technical books will be the most help, but it is interesting how many ordinary games can be useful. 'Charades' is an obvious example, as is 'Don't say a Word' (Two groups exchange a list of the titles of plays, books and films. Each person mimes one of these to their own group. No speaking at all allowed. The first group to guess all their titles correctly wins.) Another useful improvisation and mime game is, 'What are you Doing?' One actor starts miming a simple action. The next person (B) asks him what he is doing. He says something that he is not doing (e.g. milking a cow). B then starts milking a cow and is immediately asked what he is doing by A and has to say something unrelated to milking cows, such as writing a letter. This continues until someone hesitates or repeats or cannot think of anything sufficiently different – milking a goat, while performing the action of milking a cow, would be out. The person left in is joined by the next and so on, until everyone has had a turn. Once improvisations, as opposed to games, have progressed quite a long way, and people are used to improvising whole scenes, it can be amusing to give a group the first line and the last line of a scene. Without preparation, the first line is 'sprung' on the rest by one actor and the group have to improvise their way logically, naturally, without forcing things, towards the last line, which they all know, but which is deliberately very dissimilar from the first. (E.g. First line: 'Quick, that chair's on fire!' Last line: 'But, you know, I did hear that the professor's wife was keen on ornithology.') Full improvisations can themselves be the object of a workshop, as can telling a story, creating a sketch, a mime sequence, or creating a character. You will have to experiment with patience and imagination.

All workshops should be conducted with lots of opportunity for talk-back and reflection on individual reactions to exercises. This is not to encourage criticism of one another, but to increase understanding and awareness. Sensitive coaching from the leader is permissible from time to time, but real constructive criticism of a person's progress is best made outside the context of the workshop. Don't try and get too far too fast. Acting is a highly technical art and it is not acquired overnight; it cannot always be mastered in a lifetime, though experience of life, understanding of human beings, and a knowledge of the Kingdom of God are all relevant to the Christian actor. While you shouldn't ever be afraid or too proud to learn from non-Christians in a workshop (invite a local drama teacher or actor to help occasionally), don't neglect the inspiration of the Holy Spirit. This doesn't mean that what you pray over will be good (see 'The Bad Samaritan' p. 188), but a workshop that spends some time acknowledging what its members share in Christ, will find its relationships strengthened, its barriers coming down and it will also find a group dynamic, which many in the theatre spend their whole lives seeking.

A note on licences

Most people who bought *Time to Act*, and subsequently applied for a performing licence, raised no query about the fee involved. However, since there have been some who wrote to us objecting to this payment (one letter argued that all our material was 'God's property and therefore open to free performance') and others who, it seems, avoided payment altogether, we feel obliged to explain the thinking behind the licence fee for *Lightning Sketches* very clearly. All plays and sketches published, except some educational material, are subject to royalties for professional performance (usually eight or more per cent of box office takings) and to performing licences for amateur groups. These licences often cost more for each performance than the total cost of our licence. Our intention is to charge once for a three year licence and again after three years if a group wishes to continue with the material. The licence is more than the licence for *Time to Act,* to allow for inflation and also taking into account the inclusion of more sketches and several longer pieces. Most of our readers will, we feel sure, bear with us as we explain that it is an honourable principle, 'the labourer is worthy of his hire', and both of us are attempting to make a living through writing and working in the theatre. We understand the desire of certain groups to economise as much as possible, but please do not write asking for permission to perform 'one sketch' without paying for a licence. This frugality is sometimes in a worthy cause but the hesitation in paying the fee may lie in not accepting that artists should be paid for their work. We have chosen what we believe to be a very low fee to avoid any possible offence or misconception of our aims in publishing this material. Naturally, we hope that the appropriate licences will be paid for with due honesty. The principles involved here can – and should – be extended to the budgeting of theatre productions in a Christian context. It is all too easy to underpay people and in some cases do serious damage to the Christian witness of a church, by taking professional advice for granted. When somebody is clearly dependent on a freelance income, or their professional services are used in any way, proper remuneration should be organised.

This note only applies to a minority of our readers and we would like to thank the hundreds of groups who have written to us applying for licences for *Time to Act*, especially for the warmth of their letters and the encouragement they have given us to continue writing.

ENTERTAINING TRUTH

ONE: So what's this, then?

TWO: An article on 'Entertaining Truth'.

ONE: You're sure it isn't a sketch?

TWO: No, it's an article.

ONE: I see. You don't think there's a danger that people might start performing it?

TWO: People don't perform articles, do they?

ONE: Not usually, no. But they could be misled by the dialogue.

TWO: Not if they know it's an article.

ONE: We ought to make that clear, then.

TWO: O.K. This is an article. That should be clear enough.

ONE: It's more of a discussion, isn't it?

TWO: Look, we're just wasting space now. Don't start splitting hairs.

ONE: Is that 'hares' or 'hairs'?

TWO: Look . . .

ONE: I suppose there is a certain informality this way.

TWO: Yes, it's worth a try. So where do we start?

ONE: Coffee?

TWO: Please.

ONE: The word play on 'entertaining' in the title raises some interesting questions.

TWO: Hopefully, yes.

ONE: For a start, I think there are a lot of people who would say that you can't mix 'truth' with 'entertainment', because they see entertainment as being essentially frivolous and therefore a poor vehicle for the truth about God and the world. A sermon would seem to be more appropriate.

TWO: And yet all good sermons have to be entertaining up to a point, or people would just switch off. Jesus, of course, entertained his listeners with parables, and even in the most important aspect of his work – the redemption of the world – he wasn't just *talking* about God's plan, but he was the total embodiment of it; he could be *seen* and *touched*, as well as heard. Jesus told the Parable of the Vineyard about his own death at the hands of the Jews – a prophetic entertainment, if you like. The truth of the story was perfectly clear to his audience and he was almost arrested on the spot, but the deeper truth that lay behind the story wasn't fully apparent until Calvary, when it was acted out for all to see.

ONE: But this distinction between the truth of the story and the truth (the historicity) of the events described in the story is important. Whereas the parable is an imaginative and entertaining way of showing what will happen, Calvary shows it actually happening. These two levels of truth (the entertaining and the historical) are obviously inextricably linked; at the time, the telling of the parable itself very nearly precipitated the events of the crucifixion. However, surely both the parable and the dramatic action of God's death on the cross are a very long way from what is normally meant by 'entertainment', despite the number of imaginative, visual or dramatic elements they may contain?

TWO: Of course, but if to 'entertain' simply
means to give as much thought to *how*
something is said, as to *what* is said, then
these elements are not just superficial;
they are intrinsic to all effective communication, whether one is talking about
God's communication to man, or man's
communication to man. Words alone
have never been sufficient.

ONE: We still have to be careful of connotations
here –

TWO: Yes, they can be very nasty.

ONE: Thank you. Ideas and truth can be
'entertain*ed*'; they can be expressed in
ways which are either dull or 'entertain-
ing', but 'entertain*ment*', certainly if we
are thinking of the theatre, usually refers
to something 'unreal' or imaginative, like
the parable. This is often where the
problems start, especially as the word
'entertainment' carries some bad
associations.

TWO: But in and of itself, there is nothing wrong
with it, like anything, it *can* pander to the
worst human instincts and trivialise the
truth, but it can also be inspired by a love
for people and a sense of humour which
can enhance our understanding of ourselves, of the world and of God. The
question of unreality needs some explaining. A painting could be considered
'unreal', but we all hang pictures on our
walls which are not only decorative, but
also express and remind us of things
which are true about life. For all its
'unreality', Rembrandt's painting of the
Crucifixion probably helps us to understand more about the meaning of that

event, than if we had actually witnessed it. For instance, he paints himself into the scene, because he is also responsible for Christ's death.

ONE: The same could be said of a play, in that, while we know we are watching an 'unreal', rehearsed performance, the truthfulness of its content can still have a deep impact on our lives. The content is not destroyed by the imaginative form, but can be highlighted and clarified by it. On the other hand, there are limits to entertainment. Take the issue of evangelism, for example, where the object of the communication is to help people to come to know God and his forgiveness for themselves. An entertaining sketch or play, like a parable, can be an important, even crucial step along the way, but it will inevitably stop short. People come to Jesus through the direct intervention of the Holy Spirit, and by being convinced by Christians testifying to the reality of God in their lives. Christian actors and entertainers can, through their art, express the truth of the Gospel, but there will still be that moment when a member of the audience, to whom the performance has spoken, needs to say to one of the cast, 'What you're saying makes sense, but is it actually true in your own life? Do *you* believe it?' – a bit like the man who came to Jesus and said, 'Lord, I believe; help my unbelief.' Hopefully, that person would soon be talking to God 'face to face' and that would be the real moment of truth, but the significance of the entertainment in getting him to that point, shouldn't be undervalued – one of many possible steps along the way. In evangelism, personal testimony is fundamental; an actor can only speak for the character he is acting, rather than for himself. Did you want to say something?

TWO: No, I'm very happy to listen.

ONE: Feel free to chip in anytime.

TWO: I will, I will. (*Pause*) Have you finished, then?

ONE: For a bit.

TWO: Well, what about considering another primary way in which God communicates to man? Through the beauty of Creation, for instance. 'The heavens are telling the glory of God and . . .'

ONE: Psalm nineteen.

TWO: Oh, yes. 'And there is no speech, nor are there words, yet their voice goes out through all the earth.' God didn't need to put texts on the rose petals, or verses coming up like credits on sunsets in order to explain things. Creation speaks its own language which captures our attention, delights our senses and reveals to us the nature of God. In many ways, Creation itself is entertaining. There's another creation passage in Proverbs, which describes Wisdom, who is often seen as a personification of Christ or Truth, as 'ever at play' before God. This idea of 'playing' and relaxing in the created world is surely included when Jesus told us to become like children in order to enter God's Kingdom. And just as play is a 'serious business' for children, so playing and entertainment for adults can have much more significance than merely passing the time.

ONE: So entertainment is a serious business?

TWO: It can be, yes. A play can be as serious as a sermon.

ONE: This might be a good point to end on, because we're almost back where we started – the difference between a play and a sermon.

TWO: We should try and avoid the impression of going round in circles.

ONE: I suppose one could say that a play and a sermon had a similar relationship to a love-poem and a love-letter. The love-letter, however eloquent, has a specific intention, to communicate the feelings of the writer and to elicit response from the lover. The love-poem, on the other hand, is far less likely to elicit specific response but will, if it is good, deeply enrich the reader's knowledge of love.

TWO: Both are valid forms of communication and both are stronger if they are speaking the truth.

ONE: And if they're entertaining.

TWO: True.

ONE: Is that it, then?

TWO: Well, we seem to have scratched the surface.

ONE: Yes, sorry about that. I'll try and get you a new one.

TWO: More coffee?

TRUE TO LIFE

The aim of this section is to communicate through the life of the characters more than through a particular 'message'. There is a need to develop beyond 'two-dimensional' communication, without denying its value, by breathing as much vitality and independence into the characters as possible. The characterisation is only tentative in some of these sketches, but marks a beginning. The short play included, 'A Funny Thing', is an invitation to our readers to develop their skills in performance by producing more ambitious material.

Early One Morning

LUKE, *a doctor*; SALOME, *his housekeeper*; MARY, *a young girl*

This sketch is based on the appearance of Christ to Mary on the morning of the resurrection. For a full discussion of the material see the article 'Writing Sketches'. LUKE *is slightly donnish – a man of letters with a preoccupied air, but kindly.* SALOME *is his garrulous housekeeper, a nuisance at the best of times but on this occasion – the most tense weekend in the household of* LUKE *in memory – particularly aggravating.* MARY *is a local girl, simple-hearted and down to earth. She speaks with a slight Liverpudlian accent (or one appropriate to the region of the performance). The sketch should be performed in modern dress.*

Enter LUKE, *followed by* SALOME. *He carries several books towards his desk. He is clearly agitated as he thinks back over the events of the weekend, but controls his frustration with* SALOME, *who talks continuously.*

SALOME : I knew it would come to this, that's all I'm saying.

LUKE : Quite. You've made your opinion clear.

SALOME : I mean, that young girl Mary, well . . . It doesn't bear thinking of, does it?

LUKE : No, I'm sure you're right there, Salome. Now if I can just have a few moments peace?

SALOME : Going off into the night like that to who knows where, I wouldn't presume to say, with what she done in her past life . . . A young girl like that, selling her body for sex, it's too shocking to mention, all those men and those –

LUKE : What are you driving at, woman?

SALOME : Well – gone, just like that. Into the night.

I went to clean her bedroom and the bed wasn't even slept in, imagine that, and all her best perfumes were gone from the dresser. And I put two and two together.

LUKE: Yes, I'm sure you did, Salome. Now will you leave me alone, please?

SALOME: All I'm saying is, Doctor, all I'm saying, with respect, is – after what you've done for her, taking her in after her sordid past life and making a home for her and giving her a job and making a respectable woman of her – after all that, as soon as that Jesus is dead and gone, off she goes without so much as a by-your-leave back to who knows where? It doesn't bear thinking of, does it? I mean, who knows what she might be up to even now with all them –

LUKE: (*Almost losing control*) Salome. Mary has changed. Mary is a very nice girl. Whatever may have happened in the past, that doesn't matter. I don't care and I don't want to hear about it.

SALOME: But what about the perfume? I mean, why the perfume? That's all I'm saying.

LUKE: For heaven's sake, woman, get on with your cleaning and leave me alone.

SALOME: I told you this Jesus business would come to a sticky end.

LUKE: *Jesus was God!* (*Silence*).

SALOME: That's as maybe, but we've all got to go on living our lives as before.
(*Enter* MARY. *She is dressed casually, but prettily. Her hair is a jumble, her face radiant. She has been running but stops suddenly, seeing their faces. She holds a small bunch of flowers*)

MARY: Hello.

SALOME: Now where have you been, young lady?
I was worried to death I was, sick as a
dog. Off in the night like that, what have
you got to say for yourself?

MARY: I've brought you some flowers.

SALOME: (*Stricken with embarrassment*) Oh, well.
That's a nice thought, dear . . .

LUKE: (*Gently*) Where have you been, Mary?

MARY: In the cemetery.

SALOME: A nice young girl like you in the cemetery,
whatever next?

LUKE: Mary . . . going to the cemetery won't
bring him back to life and we must . . . all
go on living our lives as best we can.

SALOME: That's right, just like he says, we've got to
make the best of it.

LUKE: (*Increasingly sympathetic*) I understand
how you feel . . . I've been searching the
scriptures all night, but no joy. (*He points
despairingly to the books*) I can't make
sense . . . why it should have to happen
. . . I don't know why . . . if only he could
be here to explain himself, but . . .

MARY: Yeah, well, I've just seen him in the
garden.

LUKE: Mary, I've got one or two bottles of
medicine in my bag which you may find
helpful. I sometimes take them myself
when I'm under stress. (*He opens his bag*)

MARY: I've just seen Jesus! I thought he was the
caretaker –

LUKE: The caretaker?

SALOME: Well, there you are. The caretaker. I
mean. Hallucinogenics, that's it.

MARY: I said, 'Where've you put the body?' 'Cos
the grave was empty. You know, just a
hole. Just a big, black, empty hole and no
body.

LUKE: (*Noting down her symptoms*) I see, I see . . .

MARY: And I said, 'Hey, where's the body gone?' Thinking he was the caretaker –

LUKE: (*Nodding*) Uh-huh, uh-huh . . .

MARY: And he said – and I was crying so much I couldn't see who it was, you know what I mean? – He said, 'Mary.' And before I turned I knew . . . I was just in floods of tears, I was so happy.

SALOME: Could be sunstroke.

LUKE: (*Taking the matter in hand*) Mary. Let me be frank with you. You've had a traumatic experience in losing your best friend, we've all been deeply shocked. And in a certain sense, I think what is happening in your imagination has an element of truth for us all. In a certain manner of speaking, yes, Jesus is still with us . . . his, er, words and, of course, the memory of his actions . . . live on . . . and, in a deeply symbolic way, I think one can say, Jesus is, for want of a better expression, alive.

MARY: *I've just seen Jesus!!* I've seen him with my own eyes. Just now. Half an hour ago. He said, 'Hello, Mary', I said, 'Hello, Jesus.' He was there. I was there. We laughed and cried. And you won't find that in your books because it doesn't happen very often.

SALOME: The girl's deranged. Totally.

LUKE: (*Confidentially, to* SALOME) The point is, Salome, if the impossible were to happen and Jesus was to rise again from the dead (*glancing over his shoulder at* MARY, *who seems to be praying or gathering strength*) I don't think he would appear to Mary first.

MARY: (*Overhearing*) Oh, I see, I don't count.

LUKE: (*Blustering*) No, no . . . don't get me wrong, it's just that . . . you're a woman, and, well, women do get sort of over-wrought and er . . . (*gesticulating nervously*) sort of get the wrong end of the stick, you know.

MARY: And which end of the stick have you got then?

SALOME: (*Taking* MARY *by the arm*) I think the Doctor's got a point here and what's more, Jesus is . . . well, he's passed on now . . . and it's best to be sensible. That's what I say, be sensible like a good girl and come and have a nice lie down . . .

MARY: (*Desperate*) *Jesus has risen from the dead!!* I've seen him . . . I . . . (*Freeing herself from Salome*) It's impossible and yet it happened . . . How can I tell people what I know to be true? (*Exit* SALOME) Oh, Lord, you've put me in a very difficult position, you know . . .

Question Time

JOHN, *the disciple*; PETER, *the disciple*; NORMAN, *man in his early forties*; JANE, *his girlfriend, somewhat simple-minded and younger than Norman*; VOICE OF JESUS

Many people feel a strong empathy with the disciple Peter, who was a very honest man and had a deep love for Jesus. His triple denial of his Master is therefore an agonising moment in the gospel story. Peter's nerve failed him during Jesus' trial, but his failure was forgiven and healed later by three questions put to him by Jesus in that moving incident beside Lake Galilee, recorded in John's gospel. This sketch brings those two occasions together and tries to show the pressures of discipleship as well as the depth of love which surrounds the disciple.

The scene is set in a pub near the courtroom where Jesus is on trial. JOHN *and* PETER *are seated at a small table, on which there are two half-empty beer glasses and an ashtray.* NORMAN *is a rather dull, suburban character, although he covers this with a forced bonhomie.* JANE *retains an air of the dolly-bird. She is self-conscious and very taken with* NORMAN. JOHN *and* PETER *are talking intensely and secretively.*

> JOHN: Peter, where on earth can I get three camels at this time of night?
> PETER: Go and see Simon on Market Street.
> JOHN: OK. Well, what do I do when I've got them?
> PETER: Bring them back here and hide them round the back of the pub. We'll wait until the trial's over. They'll bring Jesus out with a guard, one in front and one behind. We'll have to take out the guards, grab Jesus and make a run for it.
> JOHN: If the camels haven't made a run for it

first.

PETER: Look, we've got to do something! What else can we do?

JOHN: I don't know.

PETER: Honestly, I would do anything – even if it means getting killed.

JOHN: You've said that before. To Jesus. We all said it and there's two of us left now.

PETER: So it's up to us, then.

JOHN: He said we'd all run away.

PETER: Well, we haven't, have we?

JOHN: What about you denying him before cockcrow?

PETER: Oh, rubbish. He just said that because he was tired and upset. He's bound to expect the worst. We can get him out of this.

JOHN: We can try. (NORMAN *and* JANE *are coming over to their table, carrying drinks*)

PETER: But we must have those camels!

JOHN: Ssshh! OK. I'll be back in ten minutes.

NORMAN: (*Sitting opposite* PETER) Not in a hurry, is 'e, your friend? (JANE *sits down*)

PETER: Mm?

NORMAN: Won't get far out there. There's that many people pushing and shoving, with this trial going on.

JANE: Oooh! It's murder. We just come out for a quiet drink.

NORMAN: Certainly stirred up some strong feelings, anyway.

JANE: Yeah.

NORMAN: Can't think why. I mean, we've seen 'im around before, preaching and that. Seemed fairly harmless. Always had a bit of a following, but nothing to get steamed-up about.

JANE: No.

NORMAN: Do you know much about this trial, then?

PETER: Mm?

NORMAN: The trial. Do you know anything about it?

PETER: Not a lot.

NORMAN: Oh. (*Pause*) What do you do, then?

PETER: Fish.

NORMAN: (*nonplussed*) No, I mean, what do you do for a living?

PETER: Fish. I fish.

NORMAN: Oh, FISH! Sorry, I thought you just said 'Fish!', you know. I see, you catch . . . fish.

JANE: In Jerusalem?

NORMAN: Yeah, you won't catch many fish round 'ere, mate. They only catch sharks here, like that Jesus feller. Poor blighter. (*With laboured good humour*) 'Ere, when is a fish not a fish? (PETER *doesn't react*) When it's a plaice. (HE *and* JANE *laugh*) Like it? Plaice? No, seriously, what *are* you doing here?

PETER: Well . . . I'm on holiday.

NORMAN: Oh, yes. Angling for a few other things, eh? Say no more.

JANE: Oh, don't.

PETER: Just a holiday.

NORMAN: Where do you hail from, then?

PETER: Galilee.

JANE: That's nice. That's where this Jesus bloke comes from.

PETER: Oh, does he?

NORMAN: Surprised you not knowing that. They say he's more popular up there than what he is down here.

JANE: You must've 'eard of 'im.

PETER: Oh, yeah, I've heard of him.

JANE: Hang on. Haven't I seen you before somewhere? There was a picture of you in the paper.

NORMAN: That's right. With Jesus. Day before
yesterday.

JANE: You're not letting on, are yer?

PETER: Must be my twin brother.

NORMAN: Oh, come on, Mastermind. Spill the
beans.

JANE: Go on.

NORMAN: 'Ere, 'ere, name? (*Silence*) Occupation?

JANE: (*Joining in the joke*) Fisherman.

NORMAN: Right. You have two minutes to answer
questions on fishing, with special reference to Jesus of Nazareth, starting *now*.

PETER: What are you on about?

NORMAN: (*Enjoying himself*) What's this Jesus like,
eh? Good at fishing?

JANE: (*Smirks*) Pass.

NORMAN: Did he ever preach from a boat?

PETER: Look, leave it off, will you. I don't know
him.

NORMAN: Not scoring too many points, are we?
Would you say that Jesus was tall, dark
and handsome, or just soft in the head?

PETER: What is this? I don't know who you're
talking about!

NORMAN: (*Suddenly clucking like a chicken*) Don't
shoot. Don't shoot! I'm only asking.
Come on, you can tell us. He's friend of
yours, isn't he?

PETER: I'm telling you, *I don't know him!* (PETER'S
*vehemence provokes a brief cacophony of
chicken noises from* NORMAN *and* JANE,
ending with the sound of a rooster. PETER
stares. JANE *and* NORMAN *laugh mockingly*)

NORMAN: Our part-time fisherman's not taking the
bait, is he?

JANE: Maybe he's chicken. Come on, let's go.
(*They rise*)

NORMAN : Sorry, mate, didn't mean to rock the boat. (*Pause*) 'Ere, what did Neptune say when the sea dried up? Mm? I haven't a notion. Get it? A notion. Ooh, dear, no sense of humour, these Galileans . . . (*Exeunt* NORMAN *and* JANE. *Their laughter fades away.* PETER, *left alone, breaks down. As if from inside his mind we hear the* VOICE OF JESUS.)

VOICE : Peter, do you love me?

PETER : Jesus. You know I love you.

VOICE : Do you really love me?

PETER : Lord, *you* know that I love you, but I just . . .

VOICE : Do you really *love* me?

PETER : (*There are tears in his eyes*) Yes, I do. You know I do. (*Enter* JOHN)

JOHN : Peter, I couldn't get them. What's the matter? Peter? What happened? (PETER *is too choked to speak. He turns to look into* JOHN'S *face. The lights fade to blackout*)

Prince of Peace

JONATHAN, *a Zealot from Jericho*; HANNAH, *a young Zealot, also from Jericho, who has been brought to Jerusalem by Jonathan, because she has just killed a Roman soldier*; SIMON *and* ANNA, *married. Zealots living in Jerusalem*; MATTHIAS, *Simon's brother*; NATHANIEL, *Simon's father, now an old man*

Scene: Jerusalem, shortly before the birth of Christ. A room in SIMON'S *house. Evening.*

This sketch may be an encouragement to those who are regularly faced with the task of writing new material, since the script was produced on the basis of a group improvisation. The improvisation lasted for about twenty minutes and was then reduced to a five-minute piece. Each actor prepared their own character on the basis of an outline given by the director and also knew the main details of the plot. The result feels as if it might be a scene from a longer play and should be approached with that in mind in performance. The actors should spend time thinking through the background to the scene and to their characters in order to give integrity and conviction to the whole piece. By focusing on the militancy of the Zealots, this sketch provides an unusual angle on the Christmas story – the coming of the Messiah.

SIMON, MATTHIAS, HANNAH *and* JONATHAN *are arranged around a living-room, some seated, some standing. Towards the back of the stage is a table, on which is a large book.* NATHANIEL *is seated near the table. The scene opens abruptly, to give the impression of cutting in on a longer conversation.*

> JONATHAN: It was an accident. She didn't mean –
> MATTHIAS: Accident! You don't murder people by accident.
> JONATHAN: A mistake, then.

HANNAH: Look, I've said I'm sorry.

MATTHIAS: Saying sorry won't make the body of a Roman soldier vanish into thin air, will it?

SIMON: Calm down.

JONATHAN: We did hide the body afterwards, but they're bound to know he's missing.

SIMON: Were you followed out of Jericho?

HANNAH: I don't think so. But there were several of them on the patrol when I killed him.

MATTHIAS: Lured him round the corner for a kiss. You're so cheap. You don't think, do you?

HANNAH: And what do you do? What do we all do, all the time? Sit. And think, and plan. Hatching up wonderful schemes to overthrow the Roman Empire, when the truth of it is, all we're doing is whispering in darkened rooms and giving each other meaningful little nods if we happen to pass in the street. Some revolution.

SIMON: (*After a pause*) They won't let the matter drop, when they can't find you.

JONATHAN: There are bound to be reprisals. They could pick on anybody.

MATTHIAS: Exactly.

HANNAH: We've got to start somewhere. We need a show of force.

SIMON: We're not ready for it yet, Hannah. At least half our people in Jerusalem have had to move out into the hills.

JONATHAN: Jericho's not strong, either.

HANNAH: The longer we wait and do nothing we'll never know how strong we are. You don't recruit an army by waiting.

MATTHIAS: Nor by ridiculous gestures of resistance that make life impossible for everyone. Of course we must wait. The Jews have

always waited for the Messiah to come;
that's what this whole nation is about.
Ask Father. His generation has suffered
more than you ever did and has learnt the
patience that God will honour.

SIMON: The Messiah will come to lead us when
we are ready.

HANNAH: The Messiah will only come when we
show that we're prepared to fight.

NATHANIEL: The Messiah will come, (*They look at him
for the first time*) without your conditions.

JONATHAN: The voice of patience, as always. (*Enter*
ANNA)

ANNA: Simon, the Romans have ordered a
census. Everybody's got to go to their
birthplace to be recorded – names, ad-
dresses, family connections, everything.
The whole of Jerusalem's in chaos.

SIMON: Who told you this?

ANNA: There was a town crier in the market-
place, but they're going to come round to
every house.

SIMON: A search?

ANNA: Probably. You can't stay here, Hannah.

MATTHIAS: She'll have to go and join the others in the
hills.

HANNAH: Oh, thank you very much.

MATTHIAS: Well, what else can we do? It's your own
fault.

JONATHAN: I could take her there on my way back to
Jericho.

ANNA: You'll have to travel tonight.

JONATHAN: With everyone tracked down, recorded
and filed away, it's going to make our
activities almost impossible.

SIMON: It'll be far more dangerous.

HANNAH: And we'll go on waiting, just as before;
cowering in caves in the hills.

MATTHIAS: (*Who has picked up the book. Reading*) 'I trod the peoples in my anger and trampled them in my fury; and their life-blood is sprinkled upon my garments and I have stained all my raiment.'

HANNAH: (*Continuing the quotation*) 'For the day of vengeance was in my heart and the year of my redeemed is come.'

SIMON: But we cannot take the Messiah's cause into our own hands.

MATTHIAS: Can't we? Listen again. 'And the greatness of the kingdoms under the whole Heaven shall be given to the people of the saints of the Most High . . . and all dominions shall serve them.' (*He puts down the book*)

JONATHAN: Including the Romans.

HANNAH: We are the right hand of the Messiah and that hand holds a sword.

NATHANIEL: (*Reading*) To us a child is born; to us a son is given. And the government shall be upon *his* shoulder, and his name will be called Wonderful Counsellor, Mighty God, Everlasting Father, *Prince of Peace*.' (*Pause*)

ANNA: Do you believe that, Father?

NATHANIEL: I don't believe the Messiah would have killed that soldier, Hannah.

A Funny Thing

'A Funny Thing' *was first presented by Riding Lights Theatre Company at The Queen's University, Belfast, Arts Festival, on 10th November 1977, with the following cast:*

SAUL	Paul Burbridge
GAMALIEL	Richard Mapletoft
ANANIAS	Nigel Forde
FLORA	Sarah Finch
VOICE	Murray Watts
STEPHEN	Geoffrey Stevenson

Directed by Murray Watts

A Funny Thing

SAUL, *a young pharisee*; GAMALIEL, *a doctor of the law and member of the Sanhedrin, former teacher of* SAUL; ANANIAS, *a Christian in Damascus*; FLORA, *a Christian in Damascus and wife of* ANANIAS; VOICE *of a child in the street*; STEPHEN, *the first Christian martyr*

This is really a short play, rather than a sketch – and should be performed with proper staging, costumes and lighting for its full effect. The aim is to explore the story of Saul's conversion with more interest in character and situation than in a particular 'message', which is normally the function of a 'sketch'. It was written and produced for the Queen's University Arts Festival in Belfast and has subsequently been staged in theatres as the second half of an evening's entertainment (in programmes of biblical material performed by Riding Lights). Sometimes, the Flora and Ananias scene can stand on its own but this depends on the theme of a service or the choice of other sketches.

A spotlight on SAUL. *He is standing alone, facing the audience.*

SAUL: We are facing a national emergency. I
want you to know that. I want you to
understand that. It is my ambition – sole
ambition – in speaking bluntly, perhaps
offensively, that no one should go from
this room blinkered. Complacency is
more fatal than outright treason. Complacency, at this time, could bring the
cherished traditions of our fatherland
crashing about our heads like so much
rubble and no one, least of all anyone in
this council chamber, will climb out of
that rubble to see the light of God's truth
again. There will be no more 'again'.
There will not be the slightest mitigating
circumstance to wrap round our heads in
the storm of God's wrath to come. With
justice it will be said: 'They saw the light.
They did not act. They invited, courted
and merited total destruction.' (*Silence*)
Brothers, I want your blessing on a blow
aimed at the followers of Jesus in Damascus from which they will never recover. I want a two-thirds majority. No.
I want a hundred per cent majority. I
want every vote in this council chamber
– priests, elders, scribes – my brothers,
my fathers in God – I want you. I need
you now. Not your approval of my
methods, only my object: religious and
national unity. 'Your hand will find out
all your enemies, O Lord, your right hand
will find out those who hate you. You will
make them appear as a blazing oven
when you appear. The Lord will swallow
them up in his wrath and fire will consume

them.' The Lord has spoken, blessed be the name of the Lord. Amen. (SAUL *bows his head.* GAMALIEL *enters and draws him to one side, away from the imagined commotion of the Sanhedrin*)

GAMALIEL : You are gifted with persuasive speech, Saul, but do not weave words into patterns.

SAUL : My speech wasn't plain enough for you?

GAMALIEL : Unfortunately, I understood every word.

SAUL : No, Gamaliel, you have not understood – for once, just once, I have the edge on you. I can see the dot on the horizon which you think is a fly, and I know is an arrow which will pierce the heart of the fatherland.

GAMALIEL : This arrow has already been shot. There is nothing you can do to deflect its path, which is why I recommend a cool head. That is all.

SAUL : Now you are saying I am hot-headed. With respect, that is the one thing I am not – I have a raging tempest in my blood, I have a hatred of blasphemy, but my head is like ice.

GAMALIEL : You were my best pupil, Saul, you must do exactly as you think fit. If you say that you see more clearly than me, then I cannot deny it. But that may not be clearly enough. For instance, in the case of Stephen the Nazarite, you obviously had insight which was denied to me.

SAUL : Stephen has no relevance. He was a blasphemer. He died. It was unfortunate that he died, but it was a necessary foretaste of the wrath of God.

GAMALIEL : That is all you have to say about the death of this man?

SAUL : Yes, I think it probably is. Oh, Gamaliel,
as always you stand apart, shrouded in
your silent observations, your hesitations,
as life rushes past you with the force of a
torrent. I propose methods which suit the
extremity of our times. I say prison,
death, only if unavoidable – as it was in
the case of Stephen – to forewarn the
other Nazarites for their own safety. I say
it's no use damming the torrent here and
there with a word and a phrase, a gentle
exhortation, we must dry it up at the very
source with all the heat of a campaign of
harassment.

GAMALIEL : As I see it, the death of Stephen was an
illegal act of mob hysteria, in direct
contravention of both Jewish and Roman
law. (*Raising his hand*) But do not let our
misunderstandings be the cause of our
division. The God of peace go with you.

SAUL : The God of peace, if we pay the price of
peace, Gamaliel – with our own blood if
necessary, God will honour such a peace.
I know he will. I know, Gamaliel, because
I know we are right.

GAMALIEL : You are the one who is right, Saul. I am
the one who is still thinking about it.
Goodbye. (*Exeunt. Light up on a room in
the house of* ANANIAS. FLORA *is lying on a
mattress, attempting to sleep.* ANANIAS *is
shifting boxes round the room, hunting
through them aggressively*)

ANANIAS : How's the time, dear?

FLORA : How should I know? It's obviously past
midnight.

ANANIAS : Have you gone and put my hammer
somewhere?

FLORA : I haven't 'gone and put' your hammer

anywhere, you know that I leave all your things exactly where I find them, which is usually on the floor.

ANANIAS: Hammer . . . hammer . . . Well, somebody's gone and done something with my hammer, which is rather annoying.

FLORA: Do you realise how late it is, Ananias?

ANANIAS: Yes, dear.

FLORA: I really can't be doing with the way you start fumbling around looking for hammers at this time of night. It's far too late for that now.

ANANIAS: That's just the point, dear.

FLORA: What?

ANANIAS: As it is so late, a few more minutes won't make any difference. Aha, I think we may be in luck here. One hammer, but no thing in it, just the head. Which is rather a nuisance.

FLORA: Have you got what you were looking for?

ANANIAS: I've got the important bit, dear, but not the thingummy which goes in it.

FLORA: Honestly, it makes me so cross that you can't get yourself organised. I've had Naomi in all afternoon with all her problems, and Lydia here in the morning, sobbing her heart out about Onesiphorus. As if that wasn't enough without being kept up all night by you looking for a hammer.

ANANIAS: (*Still looking through the boxes*) Onesiphorus? He's quite a nice chap, you know.

FLORA: (*Wearily*) Ananias, if you had the full picture about Onesiphorus, you would realise the extent of Lydia's problem.

ANANIAS: If having the 'full picture' requires listening to Lydia, dear, I think I'd settle for the abridged version. Nails . . . Nails . . .

FLORA: You men have got no idea, no idea at all. Lydia is a battered wife, Ananias, and they've been married for fifteen years.

ANANIAS: When did this start, dear?

FLORA: Last week.

ANANIAS: If I was Lydia's husband I would have battered her years ago. Dear, could I just see if the nails are here behind the mattress? (*Lifting up the mattress and rolling* FLORA *to one side*) Aha, that's a bit tricky. (*He pulls out a small box*) I think these are going to be too short.

FLORA: What on earth do you think you are doing?

ANANIAS: I am thinking of nailing up the shutters, dear.

FLORA: The shutters?

ANANIAS: Yes, and I am planning on doing a spot of barricading the door as well, if I can just find some handy pieces of wood around the place. (*Exit*)

FLORA: I've had a tiring enough day without all this. It's the limit. No wonder I've developed an awful head. (*Sounds of banging offstage*)

ANANIAS: (*Off*) What's that dear?

FLORA: I've got a terrible headache.

ANANIAS: (*Off*) This won't take a moment. (*The banging grows louder*)

FLORA: Is 'this' necessary? (ANANIAS *enters*)

ANANIAS: That's just the point, dear, it's crucial. Saul of Tarsus is right here in Damascus.

FLORA: Ananias! He's not!

ANANIAS: That's just the point, dear, he is. He and the temple guard have been here for three days.

FLORA: Good grief! When did you hear this?

ANANIAS: This evening, dear. We're in the 'hot

seat', as they say.

FLORA: (*Very suddenly*) Take the barricades off the door.

ANANIAS: I haven't put them on yet, dear, so that would be rather difficult to do.

FLORA: Well, don't put them on then. Faith. We must have faith. Let's praise the Lord.

ANANIAS: I suggest we put up the barricades and then praise the Lord, dear.

FLORA: No, we must have faith. I am sure there is a purpose in all this.

ANANIAS: Yes, dear, there is a purpose in all this, namely, to slap us all into jail. Will you pass me the hammer?

FLORA: Ananias. I have a word from the Lord. You are not to have that hammer.

ANANIAS: Don't let's start this argument all over again, Flora.

FLORA: Which one?

ANANIAS: You know, the rather trying one about deciding whether to have cheese or asparagus on our bread and you saying we've got to pray about it.

FLORA: I never did say that, it's only your imagination.

ANANIAS: I'm sorry to correct you on this point, Flora, but you did say that we had to pray about the cheese and the asparagus.

FLORA: Well, if I did, it was you who said that we shouldn't get silly about so much praying and just get on with the job.

ANANIAS: That's exactly the point I'm trying to make, dear. We have an obligation to defend our family. Otherwise we might all find ourselves in very sticky soup.

FLORA: Hot soup.

ANANIAS: Hot water, you know what I mean.

FLORA: Come on. Let's pray.

ANANIAS: I beg your pardon?

FLORA: Come on, I'm sick and tired of the way we always talk about praying and never do it.

ANANIAS: But I wasn't talking about praying, dear, I was talking about barricading the door.

FLORA: I feel that this is what the Lord wants us to do.

ANANIAS: Fine. Well you do what you feel and I'll do what I feel. (*Exit*)

FLORA: (*Praying beside the bed*) Oh Lord, forgive my husband, he means terribly well.

ANANIAS: (*Banging in nails offstage*) Oh Lord, knock some sense into my wife's head.

FLORA: Oh Lord, preserve all followers of Christ in Damascus – save us, even if it means some of us having to suffer for you.

ANANIAS: (*Entering*) Oh Lord, where on earth have the nails got to. (*He sees them on the floor and nods a thank-you to heaven*) Ah, thank-you, thank-you. (*He goes offstage, gives one final bang, returns and climbs into bed. FLORA is sleeping*) If you realised what sort of fellow this chap was, dear, we might well be thinking in terms of a natty escape through the window. We certainly wouldn't be lying in bed snoozing our heads off. I wouldn't be surprised if we're the only Christians left in the city, you know, I mean, I bet there's just bags of them roaring off to Antioch right now. And there's no need to talk to me like that, calling my name with such authority. I'm quite able to hear you, dear, if you talk normally. Quite able to hear. That's jolly funny, the room's gone very light all of a sudden. Must be some comet, I should think. No, I don't think it is – Oh

I – (*He gets out of bed and kneels*) Yes,
Lord – Oh Lord, I – Yes, Lord – Oh Lord,
I've heard what this man has done to your
people in Jerusalem – You have chosen
him to carry your name to the gentiles?
. . . Oh Lord, I – me, Lord? Oh, but Lord,
I think you should know that I get rather
lost for words when I meet important
people – I . . . I do believe that, Lord, I do
believe that you provide . . . I . . . My dear
wife is often reminding me of this, of
course, yes . . . Oh Lord, I will honestly
try and do my level best in the circumstances. This is an honour, a great honour
. . . I . . . (*He starts searching under the bed
and round the room*) Crowbar, crowbar
. . . crowbar . . .

FLORA: (*Sleepily*) Ananias, what are you looking
for now?

ANANIAS: Just tell me, dear, have you gone and put
my crowbar in the shed or something?

FLORA: How should I know? Go to sleep.

ANANIAS: Flora, I can't explain now, but I've got to
go and see Saul of Tarsus.

FLORA: (*Sitting up*) *You what*?

ANANIAS: Word from the Lord . . . 'Go and see Saul
of Tarsus'. . . I . . . um . . . He's met the
Lord on the Jerusalem road and so on,
and I've been instructed to go and see
him, if you see what I mean, and the
general idea is that I should go and talk
the gospel over with him, as they say.

FLORA: You?

ANANIAS: That's just the point, dear. Me. (FLORA *is
lost in silent praise*) Find the crowbar,
dear, *quickly*.

FLORA: (*Finding the crowbar as in a dream, with no
effort at all*) Yes, darling, yes, yes . . . here

it is.

ANANIAS: Good. Oh look, it's raining outside. Have you seen my coat anywhere around the place?

FLORA: (*Organising him as he wanders around vaguely*) No, dear, you'll have to go without a coat. I'll pray about the rain.

ANANIAS: (*Going off stage and levering off the barricades*) Don't worry about the rain, pray for Saul of Tarsus.

FLORA: Yes, darling. (*She prays, then suddenly gets up and fetches a bag*) Quick, take this. (ANANIAS *enters and takes the bag*) Food. (*They kiss goodbye. He goes. She kneels and prays. The lights fade to blackout. The scene changes to the residence of* SAUL. SAUL *is alone. The room is dimly lit by a candle, which he holds up to his eyes*)

SAUL: No good at all. (*He puts down the candle slowly and finds his way to the window*) Is there anyone outside who can help me? Hello?

VOICE: Hello?

SAUL: Is it daylight outside?

VOICE: No, sir. It's past midnight – it's pitch black except for the moonlight.

SAUL: The moon! Where – where is the moon shining?

VOICE: Up there, beyond the corner of the house.

SAUL: Ah. Ah yes. Thank you. I'm much obliged to you.

VOICE: Do you want me to take you anywhere, sir?

SAUL: No. No thank you. No, I'm all right here, I'm quite all right, thank you. Sorry to have troubled you.

VOICE: You're all right then, are you?

SAUL: Yes, I'll be all right – just a few bad

dreams troubling my sleep. I'll be all right in the morning.

VOICE: Goodbye, then.

SAUL: Goodbye. (*He turns slowly round and walks back. Some of the images that appear to* SAUL *in the following scene are imaginary – the figures handing him their coats, for example – but others, like* GAMALIEL *and* STEPHEN, *should be seen. Good lighting effects and the use of different levels on the stage – the martyred* STEPHEN *appearing high up – are the best way of directing this. If lighting is restricted, then a very dim light is best – the figures standing in the shadows*) The light and then the dreams. Damascus, I was on the road. I had papers, signatures, instructions, plans, the temple guard. I know this for an indisputable fact. And then . . . Why is this weight pressing down on me, why are you handing me your coats? (*Although* SAUL *is blind to the outside world, he sees the apparitions very clearly. He takes the coats*) Elkanah, Joel, Nathan, Eliab, Judah, Benaiah, Micah, Daniel, Jonas – your coats – your coats, please, here, Jonathan, I'll take your coat. (GAMALIEL *appears*)

GAMALIEL: The price is too great, Saul.

SAUL: I don't know what you're talking about. Joab, Zedekiah, your coats.

GAMALIEL: The price of success, Saul.

SAUL: I'm sorry, Gamaliel, I don't see what success has got to do with it. Nathaniel, I'll take care of that. Here, Joram, throw this stone for me. Bartholomew, I'm taking care of the coats.

GAMALIEL: You have to be in the centre, don't you? You have to be noticed.

SAUL: Gamaliel, I respect you as my teacher, but I do not need to be noticed. And don't think you can escape the implications of this by refusing to take responsibility – by your silence, you are responsible. I take my part, I stand up for what I believe. (STEPHEN *appears, half-naked, covered with blood*)

STEPHEN: Saul, Saul, why are you persecuting me?

SAUL: Stephen, I didn't know. Oh God, if I'd known. (STEPHEN *disappears into the shadows*)

GAMALIEL: The death of Stephen was an illegal act of mob hysteria in direct contravention of both Jewish and Roman law.

SAUL: Gamaliel, your eyes are dark.

GAMALIEL: Dark, Saul.

SAUL: Oh Christ, it's so dark in here. I never knew that my violence was directed against you. I acted according to my light.

GAMALIEL: If you say that you see more clearly than me, then I cannot deny it. But that may not be clearly enough.

SAUL: Light! Light! Light! Light! (STEPHEN *appears*)

STEPHEN: You stiff-necked people, uncircumcised in heart and ears, you always resist the Holy Spirit. As your fathers did, so do you. Which of the prophets did not your fathers persecute? And they killed those who announced beforehand the coming of the Righteous One, whom you have now betrayed and murdered, you who received the law as delivered by angels and did not keep it. (*The darkness returns*)

SAUL: Christ have mercy on me.

GAMALIEL: You are condemned by the very law you sought to uphold.

SAUL: Christ have mercy on me.

GAMALIEL: Your fine principles, your impeccable observances of the moral code, your good works have blinded you for ever. The law is your executioner.

SAUL: Death.

GAMALIEL: Darkness.

SAUL: Dark – it was the light that blinded me – a light shining around me, near me, overwhelming me.

GAMALIEL: You were blind already. The light confirmed your folly.

SAUL: Christ have mercy on me.

GAMALIEL: The best motives in the world have led you to utter destruction.

SAUL: Damascus. I was on the road, I had papers, signatures, instructions, plans, a warrant, official sanction of my policies, government approval. And then – (STEPHEN *appears with a cry, followed by*)

STEPHEN: Father, forgive them, they don't know what they're doing. Father, forgive them, forgive them.

SAUL: I didn't know – I didn't know it was you I was persecuting, Lord.

STEPHEN: Father, forgive them . . . forgive them, forgive them . . . (*His voice becomes softer as the light begins to fade*) Forgive them . . . (*The figures disappear.* SAUL *is alone in the darkness*)

SAUL: I went down to the land whose bars closed upon me for ever, yet thou didst bring up my life from the pit, O Lord my God, when my soul fainted within me, I remembered the Lord . . . I remember a great light that shone, brighter than the sun, shining around me, near me. (*The light is coming up.* ANANIAS *enters softly*)

ANANIAS: 'The people who walked in darkness have seen a great light; those who dwelt in a land of deep darkness, on them has light shined.'

SAUL: 'Thou hast multiplied the nation, thou hast increased its joy.'

ANANIAS: 'They rejoice before thee as with joy at the harvest, as men rejoice when they divide the spoil.' Greetings from Ananias and all followers of the Way in Damascus. I came in without knocking – I hope you don't mind.

SAUL: (*Touching* ANANIAS' *face*) Ananias. I was told about you in a dream. I've had so many dreams.

ANANIAS: They're over now. The Lord has sent me to you.

SAUL: Give me your hand. In all the dreams, in the darkness – I knew only one thing, Ananias. Light. Around me, not from above – not a dream, a vision – a fact. It was on the road to Damascus. Light, then terrible darkness.

ANANIAS: Brother Saul, the God of our fathers appointed you to know his will, to see the Just One and to hear a voice from his mouth – for you will be a witness for him to all men of what you have seen and heard. Receive your sight.
(SAUL *opens his eyes. Silence*)

SAUL: I imagined you differently.

ANANIAS: Did you?

SAUL: Yes, I had this picture of you in white . . . white armour.

ANANIAS: Ah, that was probably a sort of symbolic version. Sorry.

SAUL: It's all right. I prefer you as you are, just as you are. I prefer everything just as it is.

(*He looks round*) Normal, everything is
normal . . . Do you know, when I was
blind, I learnt what things were like to
touch? I hope I won't forget that. Yesterday, when I was afraid, I went to this
bowl of water and touched the coldness
of the rim and splashed my face. I was
filled with joy. All of a sudden, I remembered my childhood.

ANANIAS: 'No one can enter the kingdom of God
unless he becomes like a little child.'

SAUL: That's a beautiful saying.

ANANIAS: It's a saying of Jesus. Here, kneel by the
bowl. I don't see why we should delay any
more. Saul, your sins have been forgiven.
I baptise you in the name of the Father
and of the Son and of the Holy Spirit.
Amen. (*As he says this, he splashes* SAUL
with water. SAUL *prays in silence*) To tell
you the truth, I imagined *you* differently,
you know . . . You'll think it a bit odd
(SAUL *looks up*) but the nearer I got here,
the more ferocious you became, a bit of
the old imagination there, I think. Here.
(*He throws him a towel*) In point of fact, I
was so hot and sweaty as I stood outside
the door that I couldn't move a muscle. I
was locked rigid.

SAUL: No.

ANANIAS: Yes. Couldn't knock on the door.

SAUL: Really?

ANANIAS: No. That was the joke. So I just came in.
In the power of the Spirit – just walked in
and felt immediately at home.

SAUL: Remarkable.

ANANIAS: It was. I was quite shaken by it. It's a
funny thing, this Christian business, I'll
say that, Saul. You'll certainly find that

out. Oh, are you hungry, by any chance?

SAUL: I haven't eaten since the first day of the week.

ANANIAS: Good, well, I've got just the thing for you – fresh bread. Two loaves and some fresh fruit. Bags of fresh fruit. (*As if to explain*) My wife.

SAUL: What a remarkable lady! (*He takes the bag*)

ANANIAS: Oh, not bad, you know, not bad at all. She's pretty well in touch with things. (SAUL *offers him some food*) No thanks, I expect she'll be dishing up a pretty good breakfast as soon as I get home, you know.

SAUL: Are you sure you can't stay?

ANANIAS: Well, perhaps the odd minute or two . . . (*The lights go down very gradually on the two of them miming further conversation.* SAUL *offers* ANANIAS *bread again, and he looks round furtively and takes a piece, making a joke of it. They continue talking and eating. The lights go down to blackout.*)

GOD AND THE AUDIENCE:
SOME THOUGHTS ON THE ROLE OF A CHRISTIAN ACTOR

This article was first given as a lecture to the Arts Centre Group and then published in *Third Way* Magazine. We are including it here because it still represents our thinking on the role of the Christian actor and, although it goes very much deeper in its implications than any of the material in this book, it offers a necessary challenge to develop artistically. There is a place for the clear-cut communication of a 'message' (such as in many of the 'two-dimensional' sketches in the earlier sections of the book), and theatre has undoubtedly had a didactic element since the earliest times. But it has also had a ritual, mysterious and complex nature which demands the utmost commitment from both performers and audience. Like life, great theatre cannot be subdivided into categories. It is natural for Christians wishing to develop their art to improve the subtlety of their performance. In this way, the extraordinary diversity of creation, above all expressed in human character, can be explored faithfully, and God's greatness need not be limited by human fear. Sometimes our musical appreciation is limited to simple choruses because we are afraid of emotions which are too complex for words – but it would be a great loss to our experience of God's eternal deity if there were no symphonies. Theatre offers the same range of expression, and no value judgement between the simple and the complex is implied. The aim of the article is to suggest possibilities which are, perhaps, only intimated in the previous section of sketches.

What is a 'Christian' actor?

This inquiry immediately suggests a fundamental question: can the word 'Christian' be applied safely to any artistic process? After all, a play often has 'Christian' implications although written by an unbeliever, and may have very few 'Christian' implications although written by a believer using a biblical theme. This is because, in certain respects, a play can exist independently of its author. What is true, is true – a man could write a play which proclaims in every way the moral consequences of an action, even, perhaps, a clear picture of God's judgement of evil, but he might not believe it himself. People have said true things without believing them. But this would not make him a 'Christian' writer, any more than believing the creed would make a pornographic novelist a 'Christian' writer. If either of these were possible, the term would become debased and it would be safer to abandon it altogether. Many artists would prefer, with some justice, to avoid any label that can become meaningless in this way, yet there is no reason why the word 'Christian' cannot be applied to a human being, as opposed to an artifact, who sincerely relates his faith to his work. A Christian writer, then, could be defined as a man who binds his creative, intellectual life together with his moral actions; who not only faithfully presents a picture of God's sovereignty, his love, his mercy, but also faithfully follows the Lord Jesus Christ in his daily life. It is a very high calling, but no higher than any calling – whatever the context – that is given to any Christian. And it is only possible to achieve this intimate relationship between life and work through grace.

The Christian actor, however, is obliged to challenge a contemporary myth that dies very hard, namely, that the actor's greatest achievement is to assume a role which has nothing to do with his own personality, that has no possible moral or practical bearing on his own existence, which he can successfully discard once the performance is over. This notion is damaging to the calling of the Christian actor, which is to find a real creative wholeness in the relationship between himself and his craft.

There are many, even Christians, in the theatrical profession, who would regard this idea as cranky and fostered by a narrow religiosity incapable of understanding the true nature of their art – which makes it even more ironical that the source for such ideas comes primarily from directors like Jerzy Grotowski and Peter Brook, who make no claim to any religious convictions. Simply by investigating the nature of theatre, they may have been repelled by the shameless lack of commitment in many actors and directors. Grotowski, in particular, maintains that the actor in the modern age is vulnerable to self-inflation and this hinders any artistic achievement in his work. For this reason, he sets himself in his Polish 'theatre laboratory', although an unbeliever, to search for a concept of 'holiness' in the actor. He sees this in terms of transforming the wretchedness of the actor, a creature brought to a condition of utter exposure before his fellow men, into a state of untouchable sanctity despite his vulnerability to the world.

There is no doubt that Grotowski's theories are extremely important for the Christian actor. His ideas follow, in some ways, in the wake of Antonin Artaud, who coined the phrase 'a theatre of cruelty', meaning not violence but rather 'rigour' – for the director, the actor, and the senses of the audience – which is surrounded by theatre rather than observed from outside. As Grotowski has pointed out, theatre can exist without make-up, without set, without lights, without music, even without a text; but it cannot exist without an actor and at least one spectator. For him the relationship between actor and spectator is so fundamental to the purity of theatre, that he has followed a process of elimination in order to heighten the quality of that relationship. This contact between actor and audience is the supreme hallmark of the theatre; the live, here-and-now enaction, something never to be repeated in exactly the same way (for even if the cast never change, the audience almost certainly does.) Because of this fluctuating relationship, minute attention has to be paid to the quality of contact between actor and actor, actor and audience. The Christian actor, for his part, is responsible for exploring the nature of his relationship with the audience in the belief that each individual is a spiritual being and will one day be answerable to the Creator. He cannot, therefore, be any less concerned for those spectators than the most ardent missionary, although his role is utterly different from that of the preacher (see article on 'Entertaining Truth').

Three motivations for acting

Why then does an actor act, and particularly, why does the Christian actor act? Grotowski has outlined three possible motivations, which can be expanded in terms of Christian belief. Firstly, it is possible to act for the audience. This may sound altruistic but it is not. It can mean a kind of prostitution: the actor offers his body to the audience in the hope of gain. He has dreams of standing ovations, flowers showering down on him, Oscars and Academy awards, scintillating press notices. Such a dream world is not only pathetic but spiritually dangerous. God's holy anger is aroused by such an attitude: 'Shall the axe vaunt itself over him who hews with it?'(Isaiah 10.15) Everything we have has been given us by God; it is not for building up our self-image. The gifts of the Christian actor are for expressing in a unique way in the theatre a relationship of great depth between the actor and the audience. In order for this relationship to be truly humble and caring, the actor must avoid orientating his performance towards the audience in the sense of currying favour; he must act *for* them, but not *to* them.

Does the actor then orientate his performance towards himself – 'self-discovery'? There are many popular theories which support this motivation for the artist, and encourage 'self-expression' as the highest form of activity for a human being. But what grounds do we have to believe, as Christians, that we should engage in 'self-expression'? None at all, unless one could envisage a transformed self-expression, and even then this would mean witnessing the grace and love of God, not *my* grace and *my* love. Although the use of remedial or 'psycho' drama (trust exercises, games and improvisations directed at greater social and psychological awareness) can prove to be invaluable in breaking down barriers and building up relationships in a group of actors, there is no basis for the belief that such exercises are a kind of voyage into the interior of a personality, with the implication that *there* are to be found the resources for spiritual transformation. This is a humanistic notion.

Why then does the Christian actor act? It is remarkable that in formulating his own idea of correct motivation, from the point of view of the 'poor actor' (a very happy phrase for the Christian actor to adopt) Grotowski chooses the idea of some numinous being beyond the scope of the stage; in other words, each actor must have 'Someone' for whom he performs, a companion not seen or necessarily shared by others. It is not clear how he thinks of this – perhaps in terms of an imagined friend, lover or kindred spirit. For the Christian actor, the answer is quite straightforward: he should act for the love of God. His acting should be part of his whole existence whose sole orientation is towards God. He is on stage because the love of God has constrained him to be there. Any Christian can apply this to their own walk of life.

Christian acting means commitment

Just as fellowship with other Christians is an essential ingredient of our fellowship with God, so the relationships between a group of Christian actors both on and off stage are vital to their acting. The maximum of contact is essential. If an actor constantly hides behind a mask in every day life, if he shirks the realities of a Christian fellowship, then it is highly likely that he will express the same tendencies on stage. He will go with preconceived ideas as to how he is going to say his lines, what sort of figure he is going to cut, with no concern for any reciprocal reaction with others (very much, perhaps, as he goes to church). A Christian in a fellowship must be deeply sensitive to the needs of others, and if he is concerned about this he may learn, for instance, how not to catch any angry tone of voice from somebody else, but will seek to modify his own behaviour in such a way as to ease the other person's frustration. An actor similarly must be sensitive to minute differentiations of tone, of presence, on stage when it comes to another actor. This is one of Grotowski's most important aspects of training, but it applies equally to a Christian context. Where there is no contact, there is no development.

Christian acting, like a healthy church, is full of potential for development. Ideally, each performance should reflect this potential, however slight. We should encourage a style of performance, a type of theatre, where a 'repeat performance' is extremely hard to achieve; as hard to achieve as repeating any truly spirit-filled service of worship. If we arrive at repeat performances, in the wrong sense, of a play or a church service, it does not mean that the script or the liturgy is at fault, but the fellowship. The actor's understanding of fellowship in the church will enable him to face with far greater insight the complex problem of relationships with men and women outside the church. One of the chief blockages to fellowship is fear, and, associated with it, the fear of the means of inclusion, commitment. But sometimes it takes an act of commitment to inspire an act of commitment, an act of exposure to inspire an act of exposure. In this respect, the actor and his actions on stage will continually be a kind of example to the spectator. The actor portraying an adulterous lust – to use a strong example – is not encouraging the spectator to go and commit adultery, but is exposing the possible threat of such a lust within himself, in the hope of inspiring an act of recognition in the mind and heart of the spectator.

Good theatre has unlimited potential for the ruthless exposure of human folly, but it will also develop far beyond the categories of the simple morality play. As an art form, theatre is often no less complex than the life that creates it. Ebullient laughter – sheer joy at human eccentricities, social satire, insoluble problems of the human heart, are all an intricate part of this astonishing gift from God. The Christian actor is bound to develop such an art with integrity. He cannot give a superficial performance of any part, for whatever reason, especially out of a servile respect for the so-called religious sensibilities of a Christian audience. He must shun the world of false sentiment. Through his knowledge of God, he understands not only the nature of good but also the nature of evil. He cannot countenance performing a part in such a way as to undermine the severity of sin (or happily devote himself to a play which does so), because this would not be true to a biblical exposure of human nature. A great number of plays, however, do not underestimate evil; they make the spectator very conscious of it. This kind of exposure through acting can inspire similar exposure, of a constructive kind, in the heart of the spectator. But it is not the responsibility of the actor to see that this constructive process takes place, but of the spectator. There will always be those, perhaps the majority, who leave the theatre struggling to keep their masks intact. You cannot interfere with self-imposed blindness, any more than Isaiah the prophet could.

The Christian actor needs to be 'lost'

The analogy of Isaiah's prophetic ministry is more than a passing one for the Christian actor. God turned Isaiah from 'a man of unclean lips in the midst of a people of unclean lips' to a man of righteousness in the midst of a polluted world. Isaiah was then commissioned to preach a message which would be disregarded except by the few. Judged by worldly standards, he would be a failure as a communicator. Tradition says that he was sawn in half, a less gratifying end to his career than a life fellowship of the

British Academy of Film and Television. He is an archetype for the Christian actor because he underwent a transformation of self which led away from courtly acclaim to isolation.

God's remedy at a moment of crisis in Isaiah's life, unsure of his role, insecure at the death of the king, was to give him the most awe-inspiring vision of the King of kings. This vision of God's holiness prompted an immediate consciousness of his wretchedness: 'Woe is me! For I am lost.' He understood that he was spiritually destitute. When God appeared to him, the foundations of the temple shook and the house was filled with smoke. He was literally 'lost'. You could lay alongside this experience the 'horror of deep darkness' that descended upon Abraham in the presence of God, or the blindness that followed the blinding light in the conversion of St. Paul (see 'A Funny Thing').

'Lostness' is a vital clue in the experience of the Christian actor as the entrance to a deeper revelation of God's character, and hence of the nature of the world. While it is a temptation for any actor to build himself a repertoire of gestures, voices, expressions which he can 'pull out of the bag' when required to convey some powerful human emotion, an experience of 'lostness' discourages this kind of cynicism in his work (the same is true for any Christian minister.) We must be constantly undermining what we have done before, the words we have used (in the case of the writer), how we have spoken them and how we have expressed ourselves in the case of the actor. All this is to continually rediscover the truth about God.

One example of the theatrical application of 'lostness' is in the role of silence in the theatre. Sometimes a true contact between God and man can only take place in this way. Film, television and theatre in the modern age are more akin to the raging of the elements than the profound calm, preceding the still small voice that spoke to Elijah. The famous adage of Wittgenstein's 'whereof we cannot speak, thereof we must remain silent' is true in another sense for the 'lost' actor encountering a Truth greater than his own ability to comprehend or communicate. But, just as the gap between the fingers of God and Adam on the Sistine chapel ceiling is an eloquent expression of the inexpressible, so silence can be used creatively. A French mime artist told the authors that his father, a graphic designer, spoke ceaselessly about his art but they never communicated as father and son until his father was paralysed in an accident and unable to speak. Then, in the extremes of his 'lostness', their eyes and hearts could meet for the first time. In the context of theatrical silence, the naked contact of actor and audience, humanity and God, requires enormous courage and brilliant control from the Christian actor. It implies a great deal of risk technically and emotionally. Theatre directors like Peter Brook and film directors like Ingmar Bergman are men of iron nerve when taking risks of this kind. Christians should be no less adventurous.

The use of silence is only one small way that the notion of 'lostness' can influence an actual production. More fundamental is the state of vulnerability and therefore of acute responsiveness that it produces. Isaiah did not remain in a temple filled with smoke in the actual sense, but his experience – like Paul's and Abraham's – must have remained with him. The nature of 'lostness', which is the necessary preparation for divine consecration, implied by the 'burning coal', could be described as an overwhelming awareness of failure. The actor, by contrast, tends to have dreams of overwhelming success. At this point, when confronted by the majesty of God, those dreams are shattered.

There is a wonderful passage in the mystical treatise *The Cloud of Unknowing* which runs as follows: 'Have a man never so much spiritual understanding in knowing of all made spiritual things, yet may he never by the work of his understanding come to the knowing of an unmade spiritual thing: the which is nought but God. But by the failing he may. Because the thing that he faileth in is nothing else but God.' God reveals himself, in other words, as a God who triumphs at the moment of spiritual poverty. It is a worthwhile activity, therefore, to experience total failure as a Christian actor. This is not to suggest that the actor should invite jeers from an audience and retire pursued by rotten tomatoes, but rather that he should retire from the stage pursued by a conviction of his inability to comprehend God. If the Christian communicates easy thoughts, easy gestures, familiar concepts continually on the stage, he will encourage his audience to remain as complacent as he is himself.

Although all this might seem to apply to a particular kind of theatre, it applies equally to comedy. There is no greater mystery than the origin of laughter. (See the article 'Creating Laughter') Closely allied to self-consciousness, it is one of the primary evidences of man's spiritual nature. Any comedy actor or writer knows that great comedy is extremely hard to achieve and, when achieved, hovers on the brink of tragedy. At its height, comedy is a paradoxical form of expressing man's hopelessly earth-bound existence and his divine destiny. Great comedians are notoriously obsessed with their own inadequacy as artists and, frequently, as people. They understand what it is to be vulnerable and 'lost' better than many actors in 'serious' theatre.

A mission to express the love of God

The experience of 'lostness' – the confession of our ignorance of all things which can be expressed as the holiness of God – is the necessary preparation for Christian service. We are doomed by this vision of holiness, but the unforgettable knowledge of Christian conversion is that we are saved by the love of God. The 'burning coal' is the fusion of two extremes – the holiness of Almighty God which consumes like fire and the love of God which purifies. This touching of the lips with a burning coal conveys an experience of terrible pain which is dramatically trans-formed into healing: 'Behold, this has touched your lips; your guilt is taken away and your sin is forgiven.'

This is the orientation of the Christian actor which he

must have absolutely clear in his mind. He is loved by God and he has a mission to express the love of God. Like Isaiah, people will not understand, nor perceive, a great many things but he must go all the same. He is ordered by God not to 'fear what this people fear, nor be in dread. But the Lord of Hosts, him you shall regard as holy; let him be your fear, and let him be your dread.' (Isaiah 8.12,13) It is not the commission of the Christian actor to preach in the sense of 'winning souls'. His commission is to express a profound concern for people by not hiding anything from them about their human nature or about the holiness, judgement and love of God. His art will involve him, at times, in acting a part of a picture, perhaps a minute detail of it. Although the conventional stage has been dominated for a long time by discursive reasoning, point by point discussions, endless lengthy revelations from the 'subconscious', the art of the Christian actor is likely to lead him away from such word-based conceptions. He will know the importance of silence, of minute gestures, to convey things which cannot be put into words. He will seek to use his body to communicate feelings and thoughts which are not merely superficial; a look, a touch can communicate the love of God, as they do in daily life. In fact, he must live out this truth in his daily life or he has no hope of discovering it on stage.

Finally, the Christian actor needs to see clearly the distinction between theatre and 'showbusiness'. Acting is not a 'show-off' business, it means utter exposure before God and men. Showbusiness, in most cases, means the reverse: concealing the truth about yourself before God and men in a maze of bright lights. It is essential to understand this distinction because too many Christian artists already think they can serve God by turning spotlights on themselves. Everything should be done with God in mind rather than the audience, because this is the only way to serve both God and the audience.

APPENDIX I

Speaking in Terms (*The Breakfast Special*)

DAVID; DAVID; NICHOLAS, *soon to become* DAVID

To the uninitiated, the gobbledegook language of Christian jargon is a weird and wonderful thing; often totally incomprehensible. This is a sketch about it, and is as absurd as the language it uses. However, somewhere amongst the idiosyncrasies and the slapstick is a point worth making. A church that wishes to communicate with its fellow men slips into jargon at its peril, and also the peril of those who will inevitably give up trying to understand its message. For obvious reasons this is an extremely esoteric piece and it is not intended that it should be performed very often. The first performance was given by the authors at an end-of-term concert in an Anglican theological college, and its reception not only confirmed that jargon is a relevant target for satire, but also that one of the best ways to combat the problem is to laugh at it.

A table is laid for breakfast in DAVID'S *flat. There are three chairs.* DAVID *and* DAVID *sit opposite, leaving the third chair for* NICHOLAS *between them. Both* DAVIDS *should speak with a similar accent, which* NICHOLAS *assumes at the end of the sketch, once he has been fully processed. This accent could be done in various ways, but something clipped and precious, putting unusual emphasis on certain syllables and words (particularly prepositions) lengthening certain vowels such as 'a' (the first syllable of 'David', would sound like 'dare': Dare-vid etc.), works rather well. A large plastic sheet underneath the table is recommended.*

> DAVID 1: How absolutely super to see you, David.
> DAVID 2: Yes, it is indeed a thrilling opportunity.

DAVID 1: I welcome it very much.

DAVID 2: I find it quite helpful, really.

DAVID 1: Well, let's move on then *from* the introduction, *to* the breakfast. Do sit yourself
down, David.

DAVID 2: Right you are, then.

DAVID 1: Fire away. Perhaps you'd like to turn
with me first to the cornflakes. (*Passing
them*)

DAVID 2: Thanks for that. Er, any joy on the milk
front?

DAVID 1: Yes, let me share this with you for a
moment.

DAVID 2: Thanks for that. Now, how are things
with you these days, on a one-to-one
basis?

DAVID 1: Well, p'rhaps I could mention *three* things
on this: firstly, the Toast; secondly, Tea;
thirdly, Terrific.

DAVID 2: That excites me no end, actually. (*Pause*)
Could you pass the Tarmite, please?
(*Forced laugh*)

DAVID 1: Well, p'rhaps *before* we begin, you might
like to give us a short word, David?

DAVID 2: But.

DAVID 1: Thanks for that short word. In that case,
p'rhaps you could commit the
marmalade.

DAVID 2: (*Spreading toast*) It's funny, you know,
but people just don't see it, do they? They
just don't understand what we're on
about. It's pathetic.

DAVID 1: Absolutely pathetic.

DAVID 2: Pathetic.

DAVID 1: I'm right with you there, David. People
just don't see that they can't have the
butter and the marmalade, without the
toast.

DAVID 2: No, it just won't fit the biscuit. (*Another forced laugh together*)

DAVID 1: Well, look, David . . .

DAVID 2: Yes, David.

DAVID 1: Forgive me if I sound a little overbearing here, but could I have the butter, please?

DAVID 2: I'm conscious of that need. Don't you often need the butter at breakfast? I know I do.

DAVID 1: Amen, to that, my brother. I think this breakfast could be a really key opportunity and I'll tell you why. I'd like you to meet Nicholas, who's coming round between 08.11 and 08.32 this morning. I think you'll find him very good value.

DAVID 2: How does he stand?

DAVID 1: Pretty well-balanced, really.

DAVID 2: But you think there might be one or two things which need to be sorted?

DAVID 1: He needs to come to terms with the whole area of his Wilderness Experience.

DAVID 2: So it's been a dark time for him, but he's coming to a place of acceptance.

DAVID 1: Yes, here he is now. (*Enter* NICHOLAS)

BOTH: How absolutely super to see you, Nicholas.

NICHOLAS: Hello.

DAVID 2: So this is Nicholas.

DAVID 1: Do sit yourselves down again.

DAVID 2: You know, Nicholas, it wasn't so many years ago that I was sitting here having breakfast myself. I think you'll find there's lots of good things in store for you.

NICHOLAS: (*Lifting large box*) Well, I found the booklets which you've been sending me twice a day for the last three months, a little heavy.

DAVID 1: P'rhaps you haven't seen this one? It was

a great revelation to me – 'Breakfast with
a capital B'.

DAVID 2: I found that most helpful. But, Nicholas,
you must remember that breakfast is only
the beginning; you have to go on to lunch
and supper as well.

NICHOLAS: I've certainly been weighing up these
booklets, (*Taking out pound note*) but I'm
not sure about the cost.

DAVID 1: I take that, Nicholas, (*Pocketing note*) but
don't you think also, if we're really honest,
that there's a lesson for us in the breakfast? You see, there's no point in being
'like the porridge, dull and lumpy, but we
must be like the cornflakes, crisp and
ready to serve.'

NICHOLAS: (*Struggling to open carton*) I'm having
problems with the cornflakes, actually.
(*It bursts open*)

DAVID 2: Devastating. Absolutely devastating.

DAVID 1: Well played.

DAVID 2: Forgive me, Nicholas, but I think your
problem's not so much with the cornflakes, as with having the right balance
in your breakfast. Your priority should
be the butter.

DAVID 1: I'd just like to add, not in any way against
what you've said, David, but that's
complete rubbish. No, Nicholas, what
you need is the milk.

NICHOLAS: Could I have the sugar, please?

DAVID 1: Certainly.

DAVID 2: While that is helpful in showing us the
way ahead as you see it, David, one
wouldn't want to overbalance in the
direction of balance.

DAVID 1: The trouble with you, David –

DAVID 2: Yes, David?

DAVID 1: There's no fibre in your Frosties.

DAVID 2: (*Picking up butter*) On the other hand, what you lack is good, solid butter. (*It lands in his face*)

DAVID 1: Thanks for that. I was really struck by that, David, but there is one final thing I should like to share with you – the milk. (*Pours it over him*)

DAVID 2: I hear what you're saying, David. How do you feel about all this, Nicholas?

NICHOLAS: I was wondering if I could have the butter, actually.

DAVID 2: I think that situation's going to be covered for you Nicholas. (*Spreading him liberally*)

DAVID 1: There's a lot more to be got out of the milk jug, too. (*Pouring it on*)

DAVID 2: We've just got to get back to basics. (*Covering* NICHOLAS *with cornflakes*)

DAVID 1: Do you feel everything's coming together, now, Nicholas? (*Chucking anything remaining*)

NICHOLAS: I find it all most helpful. It's been a key opportunity – Oh, NO! what's happening *to* my voice?

DAVID 2: Oh, super!

DAVID 1: That's thrilling, really thrilling.

DAVID 2: (*To* NICHOLAS) Well done, David. Put the emphasis *on* the preposition.

DAVID 1: Well played, David. It's been good to share *with* you.

NICHOLAS: Thanks, David.

DAVID 2: Well, in conclusion, let's just bow our heads *in* porridge. (*They do*)

APPENDIX II

The Bad Samaritan

VICAR; MAN; ROBBERS; PRIEST; LEVITE; GOOD
SAMARITAN; SPECTATOR

The title of this sketch is self-explanatory. It was written to illustrate how not to write and perform sketches (see article on 'Writing Sketches') and has been staged exclusively in seminars on creative drama. Needless to say, it should not be performed in a service of worship or in any context where it would undermine the credibility of other sketches. It could be performed for fun in the context of a church party or rag concert, but any misplacing of an 'off-beat' item like this could well lead to all night prayer meetings in the church for the salvation of the drama group. The discussion points for seminars are printed in bold type.

A curtain conceals the backstage area. Assorted scuffling sounds, dull thuds and ripping noises signify the presence of the actors waiting to begin. The VICAR *walks onstage from the auditorium. He coughs.*

VICAR: I'd like to give you all a very warm welcome to the Hallelujah Drama Effort from St. Botolph's and – (*nervously glancing over shoulder to see if they're ready*) – they've come all the way from Spillingham today – (*looking round again*) – and I imagine . . . (*whispering off*) Are we ready to go? (*Beaming unctuously*) Er, in a moment or two, they'll be presenting a tableau which many of us will find, I certainly speak for myself here, many of us will find a real source of spiritual encouragement.

BAD INTRODUCTION

VOICE ONE: Who's knocked off my script?

VOICE TWO: Ssh!! **NOISES OFFSTAGE**

VICAR: And so, without further ado, I welcome the, er, (*Glancing at leaflet*) Hallelujah Drama Droop . . . Er, Group, I should say, from St. Botolph's. (*Exit. Pause. He re-enters*) I've just been asked to say that this is a dramatic rendering of the parable of the Good Samaritan.

(*Exit*) **DELAYED START**

(*Enter* MAN *who wanders around aimlessly. Silence. He whistles*)

MAN: I hope there aren't any *robbers* round here. (*Pause*) There were certainly *robbers* around here last time I walked from Jerusalem to Jericho. (*Pause*) *Robbers* have been known to beat people up. (*Pause. He is desperate*) Listen, hooves! **BAD CUES**

(*A large quantity of robbers descend on him instantly and beat him up for a very long time. Pause*)

ROBBER ONE: Hey, let's beat him up.

ROBBER TWO; Yeah. (*They beat him up again for a very long time*) **OVER-ACTING**

ROBBER THREE: Well, let's get on the horses and go.

ROBBER FOUR: Horses?

ROBBER THREE: (*Stage whisper*) He said he heard the sound of hooves.

ROBBER FOUR: What did he say that for?

ROBBER THREE: I don't know. Come on. (*He jumps on* ROBBER FOUR'S *back.* ROBBER ONE *jumps on* ROBBER TWO'S *back*) Giddyup. (*Exeunt, galloping*)

TROUBLE CAUSED BY

IMPROVISATION

(*Pause. Re-enter* ROBBER ONE)

ROBBER ONE: Hey, let's get out of here, there's someone coming. (*Exit*) **CLUMSY LINKING**
(MAN *lies groaning.* PRIEST *enters reading a scroll and trips over him.* MAN *groans because he is really hurt*)

'REALISM' OF THE WRONG SORT

(*Exit* PRIEST *and re-enter* ROBBER ONE)

ROBBER ONE: Hey, quick, let's get out of here, there's somebody else coming. (*Exit. Awkward silence. Injured* MAN *gets up and looks for* LEVITE)

GOING OUT OF CHARACTER

(*Enter* LEVITE, *struggling into costume. He delivers a completely inaudible speech*)

BAD DICTION

(*Enter* ROBBER ONE.)

ROBBER ONE: Hey, quick, let's get – (*He collides with the* LEVITE, *who is on his way out. Exeunt in confusion*) **BAD STAGING**
(*Enter* GOOD SAMARITAN, *his hands out-stretched in an awkward gesture of goodwill*)

GOOD SAMARITAN: Oh no!... Oh God, I have such a little to offer this man, but what I have I will offer him. **HACK SENTIMENT**

MAN: Who are you?

GOOD SAMARITAN: I'm the Good Samaritan.

MAN: Where are you from?

GOOD SAMARITAN: Samaria. **TOO LITERAL**

MAN: Samaria?

GOOD SAMARITAN: Yes.

MAN: But – but –

GOOD SAMARITAN: (*Kneeling beside him*) Come, I will pour this oil on your wounds. (*He searches in vain for the prop, which he has left back-stage. He mimes pouring oil*)

BAD STAGE MANAGEMENT

MAN: I don't know what to say.

GOOD SAMARITAN: (*Producing script*) Here.

MAN: Thank you. (*He reads*) Oh I am so glad you have come, I was walking down the road to Jericho, when I was set upon by robbers and they beat me up and I was lying here and first of all a priest passed by on the other side and then a Levite passed by on the other side and then you came and – (*Realises speech has finished*) – then you came.

UNNECESSARY VERBIAGE

GOOD SAMARITAN: It's all right now, you'll be safe.

MAN: (*Kneeling*) Oh God, you've saved me. (*He stretches out his hands, inadvertently poking a finger up the nose of the* GOOD SAMARITAN *who is kneeling behind him. The two actors are joined by the rest of the cast, who sing a song involving the word 'happy' at least seven or eight times. This is to illustrate* **CRINGE FACTOR**. *Further embarrassment is provided by the* GOOD SAMARITAN *who steps forward after the song to address the audience*).

GOOD SAMARITAN: We'd like to talk to anyone who's been interested in this play and would like to know more about its message to stay around for coffee and just a chat. There is a bookstall which you're very welcome to read and thank you again for having you with us. Er . . . So anyone who would like coffee at the back afterwards, would they come to the back afterwards.

SPECTATOR: (*Coming up to the* GOOD SAMARITAN) Excuse me, hello, I'm David Stephenson – I'm a drama teacher and I thought there might be one or two ways in which you could improve that sketch.

GOOD SAMARITAN : But we prayed about it.

SPECTATOR : I still think that –

ROBBER ONE : Look, we had an all night prayer meeting about that sketch.

SPECTATOR : Well, I only wanted to suggest –

ROBBER TWO : Are you saying we haven't got faith? (*The actors jostle the* SPECTATOR *threateningly*)

SPECTATOR : No, no . . .

(*Exeunt*)

FAILURE TO TAKE CRITICISM